Many Blessings to you

Sandra

Wisdom Builds Her House On Seven Pillars

Wisdom Knowledge Understanding

Sandra Crum

Copyright © 2015 Sandra Crum.

All rights reserved. No part of this book may be used or reproduced by any means, graphic, electronic, or mechanical, including photocopying, recording, taping or by any information storage retrieval system without the written permission of the author except in the case of brief quotations embodied in critical articles and reviews.

This book is a work of non-fiction. Unless otherwise noted, the author and the publisher make no explicit guarantees as to the accuracy of the information contained in this book and in some cases, names of people and places have been altered to protect their privacy.

Scripture taken from the King James Version of the Bible.

WestBow Press books may be ordered through booksellers or by contacting:

WestBow Press
A Division of Thomas Nelson & Zondervan
1663 Liberty Drive
Bloomington, IN 47403
www.westbowpress.com
1 (866) 928-1240

Because of the dynamic nature of the Internet, any web addresses or links contained in this book may have changed since publication and may no longer be valid. The views expressed in this work are solely those of the author and do not necessarily reflect the views of the publisher, and the publisher hereby disclaims any responsibility for them.

Any people depicted in stock imagery provided by Thinkstock are models, and such images are being used for illustrative purposes only. Certain stock imagery © Thinkstock.

ISBN: 978-1-5127-1733-4 (sc)
ISBN: 978-1-5127-1735-8 (hc)
ISBN: 978-1-5127-1734-1 (e)

Library of Congress Control Number: 2015917480

Print information available on the last page.

WestBow Press rev. date: 10/26/2015

Contents

Introduction ix

1. What is **Wisdom**? 1
2. How to Gain **Wisdom** 21
3. How to Gain and Keep **Wisdom** 44
4. What is the Fear of the Lord? 54
5. People who Learn This Fear Are Few 78
6. To Stand On The **Wisdom** Of God 110
7. How to Grow and Increase in the Knowledge of God 141
8. How to Discern the **Wisdom** of God 160
9. Receiving **Wisdom** In Your Life 174
10. We are to Grow up in Faith 190
11. Is it Life or is it Death 208
12. Abiding in **Wisdom** 224
13. Changes Made in us by **Wisdom** 242
14. **Wisdom** to Know When to Move, to Stand still and When to Speak 254
15. The Hidden Treasures of **Wisdom** 264

Questions and Answers 277

I am Sandra K. Crum. I am a Minister of the Gospel. I am a Teacher of the Word and a Prophet of the Lord. I have three beautiful, grown children of whom I am very proud to be their Mother. My oldest is Shellaina Miller with her spouse Tim Miller, John Merriman Jr. with his spouse Jobee, and James Merriman with his spouse Sharon. I have seven grandchildren. Then there is Michele with her spouse Mark, who I watched grow up. I am blessed to have all of my family and extended family in my life.

I was raised in a good Christian home, with very loving God fearing parents; who raised us in the way of the Lord. Their names are; James and Wilma Crum and my oldest sister Debra. We traveled and sang gospel songs as a family. We put out a long playing album when I was sixteen, called the Crum Family singers. We sang on a radio broadcast every Sunday afternoon for several hours singing and preaching traveling from church to church when we were not busy in appointments we were at our home church. Then after my sister and I were married, Dad and Mom had a surprise, our youngest sister was born Jennifer Lynn, she was a God sent to us all. Then in January 1998 God called our Father home to be with the Lord.

I would like to thank all the people in my life that inspired me to write, to help me in many ways to get this vision of mine into focus. First of all I would like to thank my Mother, Wilma Crum Thomas who read this book and told me it was very good. To Jack Thomas, my Stepdad, for giving me good advice when I needed it. To my sisters, Debra Bollack and Jennifer Beck for being there for me. To all my friends out there too many to name for giving me courage to go ahead with this book and to get it published for they cannot wait to read it. And last but not least, Doctor Jay Tackett, a minister of the Word, whom God brought into my life at the most critical time of my life. He helped me with the last two chapters by giving me this scripture and that scripture and helped me to get the wheels of my mind rolling all the more. Doctor Jay Tackett pushed me to get this done and to get it to the publisher as soon as possible for he said this was a great book of **Wisdom**.

I would personally like to thank my friend Earlene Skiles of many years for drawing the front cover of my book. I would also like to thank Pastor Billy Morton and my mother Wilma Thomas for the financial blessing for my book. In addition, I would also like to mention my friend, Sharon Stephenson for she has helped me pull this together.

The Book of **Wisdom** started out when I awoke one bright sunny morning. The Lord had put in my mind and heart the verse in Proverbs 9:1 where **Wisdom** Builds Her House and She had hewn out Seven Pillars. As the morning progressed and even late into the afternoon, the verse was still heavy on my mind. I began to ask the Lord, what he wanted me to do. He proceeded to tell me to study out **Wisdom** and her Seven Pillars. I told the Lord that I had already studied out **Wisdom** Lord! He spoke into my spirit to study it again with pen and paper. So I got a tablet, a pen, and my bible, I began to study out **Wisdom**. As the study progressed, I could not believe that I ended up with so much gleaned out of **Wisdom** and her seven pillars. This study worked into a complete book. Then I put it away and left in my folder for 18 years. One day God reminded me that it was time to get the book out and revise it. I hope and pray as you read and study this book of great **Wisdom** you glean as much as I have if not more. This is so much needed in the church world, and in our everyday lives. This **Wisdom** is very much needed in our daily walk with the Lord. **Wisdom,** as I share with you in this book, is a well spring of life springing up within your very soul.

Introduction

Proverbs 1:2
To know **Wisdom** and instruction of **Wisdom**; to perceive the words of understanding.

Proverbs 1:5
A wise man will **HEAR,** and will increase in learning; and a man of understanding shall attain wise counsels.

Proverbs 1:7
The fear of the Lord is the beginning of **knowledge;** but fools despise **Wisdom** and instruction.

Fear (Hebrew) Reverence, piety, Webster Dictionary; devotion to religious duties.
Fools (Hebrew) Foolish.

How can we express the importance of our thoughts sufficiently, in order to convey the true meaning of the Book of Proverbs 1:5? A wise man will hear will increase in learning. A man of understanding shall attain wise counsel.

The longer I serve the Lord and study his word the more I long to know him more. When I get this word planted deep into my heart, the more I understand the importance of his thoughts in his word. I am learning more every-day of my Christian walk how to incline my ears unto his word. The more word I know the more that Christ increases in me the more Adam decreases. I am learning day by day applying it to my life, I can grow in the admiration of my Lord. As Proverbs 1:5 says we will **hear** in the spirit and will increase in learning by seeking the Lord through prayer and study.

Proverbs 23:7
As he thinketh in his heart, so is he:

First a man has to think before it can become an action. Our actions speaks louder than our words as we are a direct action of our thoughts. If we think negative we will live a negative life, if we think positive we will live a positive life. Which path do we desire?

Proverbs 12:28
In the way of righteousness is life; and in the pathway thereof there is no death.

A righteous life will bring newness of life, the more word we apply to our heart the less we sin and the less death is in us.

Philippians 4:8
Finally my brethren whatsoever things are true, whatsoever things are honest, whatsoever things are just, whatsoever things are pure, whatsoever things are lovely, whatsoever things are of good report; if there be any virtue, and if there be any praise, think on these things.

Truth, honesty, are just are his way and these things will bring beauty and virtue in our lives as we learn to apply them, to have the knowledge the understanding to learn **Wisdom** and her ways.

Isaiah 33:6
And **Wisdom** and knowledge shall be the stability of thy times, and strength of salvation: the fear of the Lord is his treasure.

When we apply **Wisdom** it will give us an anchor to hold us, it will make us stable. **Wisdom** gives us strength in our salvation, as we reverence (**fear**) the Lord he will give us treasures beyond all measure.

Chapter 1

What is Wisdom?

Proverbs 9:1-5
Wisdom hath builded her house, she hath hewn out her Seven pillars:
2nd She killed her beasts; she mingled her wine; she hath also furnished her table.
3rd She sent forth her maidens; she crieth upon the highest places of the city.
5th Come, eat of my bread, and drink of my wine which I have mingled.

1. **Wisdom killed her beasts**. (Hebrew meaning) slaughtered; provide meat for the table.
2. **She mingled her wine**. (Hebrew) to mix.
3. **She furnished her table**. (Hebrew) put in order, prepared, to arrange in row, to set a value.
4. **She sent forth her maidens**. (Hebrew) young maiden, damsel.
5. **She cries upon high places**. (Webster's Dictionary) one who shouts out announcements.
6. **Come eat of my bread**. The body of Jesus Christ, come to the table eat of me.
7. **Drink of my wine which I have mingled** (**mixed**) wine represents the spirit.

Wisdom: (Greek) (Sophia) meaning; worldly or spiritually, intellectual insight, prudence, to be carnally or spiritually minded. (Hebrew meaning) Instruct, to prosper, to be skillful, make wise.

Wisdom, she hewed out seven pillars!
Seven is perfection, God's perfect number, also completion, God rested on the Sabbath (seventh) Day.
Pillar (Greek) to stiffen, a post support, covenant establish, to abide, appoint.
Hewn (Hebrew) to cut out, to dig, to divide

Wisdom (feminine) builds her house, **Wisdom** is personified for she is very wise. **Wisdom** and instruction complement each other because, **Wisdom** means skill or to be skillful, to make one wise to be **spiritually minded (To have the mind of Christ)**. **Instruction** means discipline in the (Hebrew) text. Instruction also means restraint bond, and correction. No skill is perfected without correction and discipline. When a person has skill he has freedom to create something beautiful, also when you are skillful you are intelligent and wise in the spirit and in your mind.

Wisdom Was Before The Earth Was Created:

Proverbs 8:35
Whoso finds me finds life, and shall obtain favor of the Lord.

Proverbs 8:1-5
Doth not **Wisdom** cry? And understanding put forth her voice?
Understanding (Hebrew) insight, skill, ability, discretion, reasons, **Wisdom**, skillfulness.
Mind (Greek) thinking, this is a part of the inner person that thinks and processes information into understanding, including

the making of choices, the seat where the heart, mind and imagination are located.

2nd She standeth in the top of high places, by the way in the places of the paths
3rd She cries at the gate, at the entry of the city, at the coming in at the doors.
4th unto you, O men, I call; and my voice is to the sons of man.
5th O ye simple, understand **Wisdom**: and ye fools, be ye of an understanding heart.
Standeth (Hebrew) Establishing, setting up, appointed, erected, stand upright.
Cries (Hebrew) To shout for joy, to cry plead, proclamation, call for songs, greatly rejoice, singing, triumph.
Call (Hebrew) Summon, announce, proclaim, to be invited, publish.

As **Wisdom** stands in the top of the high places, she is setting up and establishing the right standing in high places in God. (To make plain the path thereof). She shouts (**cries**) for joy she pleads to the people to come to greatly rejoice in God our Savior with singing and triumph. **Wisdom** as she calls, she summons, to announce, to proclaim, the knowledge and understanding to publish and invite all who hears to come through the doors to claim all the Lord has for us. The table is all set, the wine is mixed, the bread prepared, everything is established.

Proverbs 8:22-30
The Lord possessed me in the beginning of his way, before the works of old.
23rd I was set up from everlasting, from the beginning or ever the earth was.

24th When there was no depth, I was brought forth: when there was no fountains abounding with water.
25th Before the mountains were settled before the hills was I brought forth.
26th While as yet he had not made the earth, nor the fields, nor the highest part of the dust of the world.
27th When he prepared the heavens, I was there, when he set the compass upon the face of the depth:
30th Then I was by him, as one brought up with him: and I was daily his delight, rejoicing always before him.

As we see here how important and how vital **Wisdom** is in our daily walk with the Lord. **Wisdom** gives us life through the Word of God! Without it we cannot obtain the salvation plan, for **Wisdom** is the beginning of Knowledge. We must first acknowledge and feel the drawing of the Holy Ghost to repentance.

Proverbs 9:2
Wisdom mingled her wine.

As I said earlier mingled in (Hebrew) means to mix a mixture of wine with spices. Wine represent the spirit, the anointing is the unction of the Holy Ghost. The spices have specific meanings each one represents something. When blending certain spices together the olive oil is the binding or blending together the spices. Some spices are very expensive in the bible days, and still are today.

Proverbs 9:1
Wisdom builds her house, and hewed out Seven Pillars.

As I said earlier seven represents God's perfect number. Seven bring perfection and completion in him.

Seven also mean maturity, we must mature, to grow up in **Wisdom** in all things.

Wisdom killed her beasts. Beast can also represents our Adam nature (flesh). Man was made on the sixth day, Adam was formed out of the dust of the ground. This makes him have a beastly nature that must be killed in us. How? By being born again; Romans 10:9; by the washing of the word, by getting **Wisdom**, knowledge and understanding within our hearts, mind and soul.

St. John 2:9-10
When the ruler of the feast has tasted the water that was made wine, and knew not whence it was; (but the servants which drew the water knew): the governor of the feast called the bridegroom. 10th And said unto him, every man at beginning does set forth good wine, and when men have well drunk, then that which is worse: but thou kept the good until now.

When Christ turned the water into wine, he left the best till last. He told them to get six (number of man) pots fill them with water to the brim. Then Jesus performed his first miracle by turning the water into wine. We are the representation of the six water pots. Six the number of man, for he was; formed out of the dust of the ground on the sixth day. He filled us with his wine which represents the spirit he put in us. He filled us with the new wine which represents the spirit as he saved the best till last.

Mark 14:22-24
And as they did eat, Jesus took the bread and blessed and brake it, gave to them and said, (Jesus speaking) *"Take, eat: this is my body."*
23rd And he took the cup, and when he had given thanks, he gave it to them: and they all drank of it.

24ᵗʰ And he said unto them, (Jesus speaking) *"This is my Blood of the New Testament, which is shed for many."*

The blood represents the wine; the spirit represents the anointing, the wind of the Holy Ghost. The Holy Ghost is (Greek) (New Testament) the Holy Spirit is (Hebrew) (Old Testament) there is a difference in the Holy Ghost and the Holy Spirit. A Ghost has to have had to live before, Jesus said I must go away or the comforter will not come. The Holy Spirit in the Old Testament was only for select few. The Holy Ghost is for all who will come. The Day of Pentecost came unto the Jews and to the Gentiles. The wind of the Holy Ghost you cannot see it, but you can feel the effects of it. You see the trees branches swaying in the wind, when the leaves began to turn colors in time of autumn the leaves fall off the tree unto the ground to give the earth nutrients to heal the land, then the leaves wither away it is time to rake them up and throw them away or burn them.

Revelation 22:2
In the midst of the street (singular) of it, and on either side of the river, was there the tree of life (JESUS), which bear twelve (government, divine order) manner of fruits, and yielded her fruit every month: and the leaves (us) of the tree (singular)are for the healing of the nations.

In our everyday lives we have seasons. In our spiritual walk with the Lord we have seasons as often as the natural. The leaves in the time of autumn turn and fall to the ground. We want to run and rake them up as soon as they fall to the ground. We are not to rake the leaves till the leaves are dry and brittle. Our Spiritual leaves that fall (the word we give) on the earth, (us) gives us healing. We are in the tree of life and we are the leaves.

There is a story of a woman I encountered in a place of business. As I was sitting there in the lobby God began to speak to me. The Lord spoke into my spirit to help this woman. She did not have any means of transportation. She was on the phone asking for someone to give her a ride to the water company. I said "Lord! What do you want me to say to her?" I do not even know this woman! The Lord said: "I want you to accommodate this woman" "What! Lord I do not even know this woman! I said Accommodate her; I do not have enough gas for myself, nevertheless run around to pay her bills." The Lord said "Do what I told you to do! " "Yes Lord!" As this woman got off the phone I went to open my mouth before I could say anything she asked me if I would take her to the water company. I told her that I would take her to the water company. As I was driving she began to tell me about her lung disease and it was hard for her to walk very far. We walked into the water company together and sat in the lobby, there were windows all around the room there, she began to tell me she was facing prison in two weeks and she did not know what she was going to do. I proceeded to tell her about a friend I have that would help her, she looked at me and said "I know what you are going to say; you are going to tell me about this Jesus person" I am agnostic; I looked at her with this blank look, she looked at me and said you do not know what agnostic means do you? "No I never heard of the word" It means you do not believe in something you cannot see, Oh Ok I said. I looked out the window I saw the March winds were blowing hard. I looked at her and said: "You don't believe in the wind do you?" She looked up at me like I had lost my mind, "well yes I believe in the wind" I said "No you don't; you told me you do not believe in something you cannot see" but if you go over there and open up the door you will feel the wind, and you can see its effects, but you cannot see it." She looked at me kind of strange, I began to tell her about Jesus, she began to listen to me.

I told her if she would open the door of her heart and let Jesus Christ in she would feel the wind of the Holy Ghost. She would feel the effects, she would feel the love. I took her home with me gave her a new bible and counseled with her, by the time I took her home she gave her heart to God.

Wisdom furnished her table, she worked and prepared the table as the woman prepares a banquet for her most important guest, she invited to be there. There are invitations to send out, there is cleaning to be done, getting out the silver to polish, getting out the finest linens to iron out any wrinkles, there is a dinner to prepare for, going to the store picking out the finest food. Then prepare the foods such as baking or to cook. Then we must prepare the table, to put on the table cloth pure and white, setting the silver on the napkins to be folded just right, and to set the dinner plates. The small plates are to be set inside of the large plates the cups are to go in a certain place on top of the saucer, the glasses are to go in a certain place along with the silver; they are the salad forks, the steak knives, spoons. Everything must be in a proper setting. **Wisdom** has her table spread out for the guests are arriving.

Luke 22:30
That you may eat and drink at my table in my Kingdom, and set on the thrones judging the twelve tribes of Israel.

Twelve: Government, divine law and order.

Where is His Kingdom?

Luke 17:21
Neither shall they say, lo here! Or lo there! For behold (look) the Kingdom of God is within you!

She sent forth her maidens with the call, "The table is ready to eat of the Word of God!" We are to prepare ourselves and make ourselves ready in order for the Lord to give us His Word (bread). Are we preparing the table of our heart to the Lord or are we rejecting?

Table (Hebrew) A table spread out, a meal, to glisten (**as polished**) of stone, wood, metal, board, plate.

Proverbs 3:3
Let not Mercy and Truth forsake thee; bind them about the neck write them upon the table of thine heart.

II Corinthians 3:3
Forasmuch as ye manifestly declared to be the epistle of Christ ministered by us, written not with ink, but with the spirit of the living God; not in tables of stone, but in fleshly tables of the heart.

With the Kingdom of God within us, we have the table of our hearts prepared for the banquet dinner to partake of Jesus Christ. We are polished, tried as pure gold is tried in the fire. When we partake of the food it tastes good but as we digest it in our bellies it becomes bitter. The bitterness is choked out by the Word. The word washes us pure. When the Word get inside of us it takes all the impurities out of us. That is how the Word cleanses us, makes us clean. This is why we must prepare our hearts to digest this meal, it is sweet to the mouth but in the belly it becomes bitter for he is cleansing us from all unrighteousness.

Galatians 5:22
But the fruit if the spirit is love, peace, longsuffering, gentleness, goodness, faith, meekness, temperance.

This is what the Lord gave me in a song that I wrote back in 2004:

> The fruit of the spirit is Love, which is charity.
> The fruit of the spirit is Joy, Joy unspeakable.
> The fruit of the spirit is Peace, Peace that passes all understanding.
> The fruit of the spirit is Longsuffering, which is patience.
> The fruit of the spirit is gentleness which is kind and true.
> The fruit of the spirit is goodness, Beauty for ashes.
> The fruit of the spirit is faith, Faith comes by hearing.
> The fruit of the spirit is meekness, which is humility.
> The fruit of the spirit is temperance, for we have to be strong in the Lord.
> If we live in the spirit, let us also walk in the spirit, Looking to Jesus the Author and Finisher of our faith.

As you look here in the scriptures, the nine spiritual fruit, it only says **FRUIT!** (singular). It does not say fruits, it is one fruit, with many different flavors of attributes.

Proverbs 9:5
Come eat of my bread (Word) and drink of my wine (spirit) Representation of the Lord's last supper, of His blood, of his body.

When we go house to house to have bible study, or have a meeting, we are breaking bread (his Body), we are having communion. The Word of God is life to the soul, and to the spirit man. When the anointing is there that is the Holy Ghost; the wine. We are eating of the bread and drinking of the wine his blood. This is (symbolic) the early church actually (literally) ate real natural food at each other's house as well as spiritually.

Proverbs 9:6-9

Forsake the foolish, and live; and go in the way of understanding. 9th Give instruction to a wise man, and he will be yet wiser; teach a just man and he will increase in learning.

Let me explain this in simple terms here. When we look back from a year ago, we see no change in our walk or in our talk then we need to question ourselves here. We need to keep changing as we increase in **Wisdom**. The ministers such as: teachers, pastors, evangelist, prophets and apostles if we are preaching the same message over and over we see there is no increase in our **Wisdom** and in our knowledge then we better back up and ask God what the matter is. We should deepen in our walk and in our messages. We are never to become stagnant. God does not change but we must be constantly changing in word and deed. We are to continue to grow to mature to not be so apt to jump up every time we feel the spirit. We must learn to come under subjection of the Holy Ghost to line up with the word. We are to study the Word in order to grow in the knowledge of God. We cannot get **Wisdom**, knowledge and understanding if we do not study, (not just read) to pray to have a relationship with our Lord God Almighty. This Word comes in studying and lining up the word in order to come into alignment.

Proverbs 10:31-32

The mouth of the Just brings forth ***Wisdom:*** but the forward tongue shall be cut out. 32nd the lips of the righteous know what is acceptable: but the mouth of the wicked speaks forwardness.

These verses here are pretty well explained; a wholesome tongue brings forth life with much **Wisdom**. The righteous watch what they speak before they open their mouths, for a tongue not bridled is deadly.

Genesis 41:33: 39
Now therefore let Pharaoh look out a man discreet and wise, and set him over the land of Egypt.
39th And Pharaoh said unto Joseph, Forasmuch as God hath shewed thee all this, there is none so discreet, and wise as thou art.

Exodus 28:3
And thou shalt speak unto all that are wise hearted, whom I have filled with the spirit of **Wisdom**, that they may make Aaron's garment to consecrate him, that he may minister unto me in the priest's office.
Consecrate (Hebrew) to make holy, to be dedicated, set apart, most holy, hallowed

11 Samuel 20:14-22
16th Then cried a Wise Woman out of the city, Hear, what I say, I pray you, unto Joab, come near hither, that I may speak with thee.
19th I am one of them that are peaceable and faithful in Israel; thou seek to destroy and a mother in Israel; why wilt thou swallow up the inheritance of the Lord.

We see here not only to use **Wisdom**, but pure common sense. The Wise woman had to reveal herself in order to save herself and her household. Why are you trying destroy me, and my household? Do you know what you are doing? Let myself to reveal to you, what you are doing is; you are destroying not only your inheritance; but your own life.

Wisdom is Personified in Twenty personal Acts or Actions:

Proverbs-Chapters 8-9
1. She cries; Ministers, summons or announces.
2. She stands; setup, establish
3. She calls; proclaims
4. She speaks; to breath out, thunders, shout.
5. She reproves; to reason together, rebuke, discipline
6. She abhors; indignation, abdominal anger.
7. She admonishes; instruct, to warn,
8. She searches; examines, track down, to ransack,
9. She hates; shun enemy, an adversary
10. She counsels; sound, success, victory,
11. She advises; consider, to show oneself, approve, advise,
12. She loves; to be a friend, a lover, covenant, beloved,
13. She leads; to walk, travel, following,
14. She blesses; give praise, extol, salute, bless indeed,
15. She rejoices; be glad, joyful, cheer-up,
16. She delights; pleasant,
17. She builds; establishes,
18. She cooks; she is preparing the food,
19. She plans; she gets thing set up,
20. She invites; send out invitations.

We see all the acts **Wisdom** does and offers; we must embrace her, we must see the example she has set before us. She is useful in everything aspect of her life. She is skillful, she accepts and embraces the good, and shuns evil, she is a lover, a friend at all times. She shares blessings everywhere she goes, she is rejoice-full she give instruction to the wise man for he will learn the ways of **Wisdom**. A wise man will receive **Wisdom**'s counsel, as she advises him how to walk in success and in victory.

Proverbs 4:8
Exalt her, and she shall promote thee; she shall bring thee to honor, when thou does embrace her.

Wisdom demands attention; she wants your full attention, not part. She will bring honor to you when you embrace her to the full extent. When you exalt someone you lift them up, you give to them full honor, extol, cherish, to build up.

This is the Life Eternal; How Do We Enable this?

John 3:16-17
For God so loved the world that he gave his only begotten son, whosoever believes on him should not perish, but have everlasting life.

17th For God sent not his son to condemn the world; but that the world through might be saved.

As we see here; Jesus did not or could not condemn us, for we were already condemned. Jesus came to give life to us, not only life but eternal life. Jesus gave his life to bring and give us life. That we parish not. We are to reverence the Lord to give him honor due to him. How do we give honor to the Lord? By putting him first in our lives and asking Him to take abode in our hearts.

Romans 10:9-10
That if thou shalt confess with thy mouth the Lord Jesus, and shalt believe in thine heart that God hath raised him up from the dead, thou shalt be saved.
10th For with the heart man believes unto righteousness; and with the mouth confession is made unto salvation.

Just repeat after the pastor or minister does not make you born again or a Christian. How is that? You must not only confess with your mouth you must believe in your heart, you must have a broken heart and contrite (broken, crushed) spirit. You must know and believe you are a sinner, and you need a Savior. You must be sorrowful of your sins, and lay those sins down, and open the door of your heart to let Jesus in.

Psalms 51:17
The sacrifices of God are a broken spirit; a broken and contrite heart, O God wilt thou not despise.

II Timothy 2:15
Study to shew thyself approved unto God, a workman that needs not to be ashamed, rightly dividing the word of TRUTH!

We are not only to study the Word, we are to rightly divide the word of truth, what that means is we cannot go and take a scripture out of context. We must see the time and dispensation it is talking about, just because it says it in one place of the bible does not mean the same in another text, for it may be talking about another thing all together. This is why we have so many denominations in the world today. When you take things out of context you can prove whatever you want, but it takes the anointing to open your eyes. We must be careful, we must pray for God to show us.
Dividing (Greek) to handle correctly, guide a straight path.

I Thessalonians 4:11
And that ye study to be quiet, and do your own business, and to work with your own hands, as we commanded you.

As we study we get **Wisdom**, knowledge and understanding we learn to be quiet and listen to the Holy Ghost to led us and guide us in all truth, not part truths. Through our quietness is when we can hear God speak into our spirit. We read and study his word he also speaks to us through his word, dreams, in visions, or in prophesy, but it must line up with the Word of God. Philippians 2:12; work out our own salvation in fear and trembling. We are not to be in other people's business, all we are to do is preach and teach the word. Not to condemn one another, God loves us all where we are at.

James 3:13
Who is a wise man, and endued with knowledge among you? Let him shew out of a good conversation his works with meekness of **Wisdom**.
14th But if ye have bitter envying and strife in your hearts, glory not, and lie not against the truth.
15th This **Wisdom** descendeth not from above, but is earthly, sensual, devilish.
16th For where envying and strife is there is confusion and every evil work.
17th But the **Wisdom** that is from above is first pure, then peaceable, gentle, and easy to be intreated full of mercy and good fruits, without partiality, and hypocrisy.
18th And the fruit of righteousness is sown in peace of them that make peace.
Intreated (Greek) submissive, obedient, compliant.

Proverbs 1:5
A wise man will hear, and will increase learning; and a man of understanding shall attain unto wise counsel.
Attain (Hebrew) Branch, rod, a measure of length, a balance, to buy, to purchase, recover, redeem.

We are to attain (recover) **Wisdom**, we must uncover the Word of God. We must possess the Word; to lay claim to the Word or to own it with everything in us. For we have been redeemed (purchased) by his precious blood, we have been bought, purchased by and through the precious blood of the Lamb. We have been bought with a great price, the price of our Lord Jesus' blood. The only thing he bought or was purchased was MAN! The bible said we are to have an understanding; we are to recover to increase in learning daily his precious Word.

I Corinthians 5:19-20
What? Know ye not that your body is the temple of the Holy Ghost which is in you, which ye have of God, and you are not your own?
20th For ye are bought with a price: therefore glorify God in your body, and in your spirit, which are God's.

Well I would expound on this scripture, but it is pretty well self-explainable here. We see here we are bought with a very great high price, the price of Jesus' crucifixion.

Proverbs 11:1
A false balance is an abomination to the Lord; but a just weight is his delight.

Let me explain this scripture here a little bit more. A lot of times we hear people say, it is got to be right for it feels good, it looks right; but it must line up with the Word, or it is nothing more than witchcraft seducing spirits, lustful spirit to entice you. Go to Revelation 2:20-23; Jezebel is powerful; she is; seducing spirits, witchcraft, power control and manipulation. Jezebel is powerful, she is: seducing spirits, witchcraft, power and control. She manipulated the people and she gives illusions, she lies, draws in prophets in her web of deceit, for she is very evil. She will deceive the very elect if possible. This is why we must know the Word, eat the Word, to rightly divide the Word of truth. We will be deceived and destroyed for the lack of knowledge, for the lack of **Wisdom** and not enough truth to sustain you. We cannot go by feelings only, we must go by the Word, the Holy Ghost is what leads us guides us in ALL TRUTH! We must have a balance, we must weigh the Word to line it up or we will err in the Truth and be lead astray with her seducing spirits, it is alive and well in the secular church world, we must destroy the spirit of Jezebel, she has rocked the church to sleep, the church is in deception, thinking they are alright. They are in the comfort zone. The church in its condition has let America down! For America has forgotten God! The church cannot help America for they have lost their first love.

Amos 6:1
Woe to them that are in ease in Zion, and trust in the mountain of Samaria, which are named chief of the nations, to whom the house of Israel Came!

I Kings 9:7
And thou shalt smite the house of Ahab thy master, that I may avenge the blood of all the servant of the Lord, at the hand of Jezebel!

I John 4:1
Beloved, believe not every spirit, but try the spirits whether they are of God; because many false prophets are gone out into the world.

See the importance of **Wisdom**, to have a balance; not everyone that says Lord is got it, or genuine. We must know the spirit.

We are to try the spirits to see if they are of God. We are not to indulge in the spirits, we will get ourselves in trouble, we are to try the spirits if it does not line up then it is not of God.

Ephesians 6:13
Wherefore take unto you the whole armor of God, that ye be able to withstand in the evil day, and having done all, to stand.

This is a must! We must put on ALL the armor or we will fall under the attacks of the enemy. He will come to deceive us, tell us parts of the truth, to twists the truth as he did with Eve in the Garden of Eden. The enemy knows the word, he will quote it to us but only in parts to suit him, he makes it sound good, he makes its feel good, we are to be aware of Satan's devices.

Notes

Chapter 2

How to Gain Wisdom

Seven Pillars Hewed Out:

1. **Incline thine Ear Unto Wisdom:**

    Incline (Hebrew) to spread out, deliver, cause to yield, extend, and to give heed, hearing attentive.
    We are to yield to the Holy Ghost, to open our ears to the voice of God. Are we listening to our own spirit? Or are we listening to the Holy Ghost?

    Joshua 24:23
    Incline your heart unto the Lord God of Israel.
    24th The people said Joshua, the Lord our God we will serve, and his voice we will obey.

    When we *incline* (hearing, yield) our ears, we are yielding to the Holy Ghost, we are extending ourselves as we are hearing with our spiritual ears. As we incline our ears and incline our hearts we will serve the Lord with all our heart, mind, and soul. We will serve the Lord whole heartedly. We cannot go any further in our walk with the Lord until we first incline (give heed) our ears and our heart to the voice of the Lord, then He will deliver us, open us up in the Spirit. We need to give heed unto the Lord. We are to yield ourselves, open our heart unto him so he can do His perfect will in us.

2. **Apply Thine Heart to Understanding:**

Proverbs 2:2
So that thou incline thine ear unto **Wisdom**, and *Apply* thine heart to understanding.
Apply (Hebrew) abide, incline, stretch out, entrance, abide, attain, employ, regard, a dress (as to put on) attire.

When we apply our heart to understanding we are applying it as we would be putting on a garment, or applying makeup, it becomes part of us. Applying our heart; is what the Lord is telling us to do John 15:4. We abide in him and He abides in us we become inseparable. Apply is to take and run with it, it is yours to have and to keep. Ephesians 6:11: We are to put on the whole armor of God to be able to stand against the wiles (tricks) of the devil. We must put on the garment of salvation. We must apply our hearts to understanding the Word of God, not man's understanding, but God's understanding. Proverbs 3:5; Trust in the Lord with all thine heart; and lean not to thine own understanding.
Understanding (Hebrew) intelligence, skillfulness, **Wisdom**.

When we understand **Wisdom**, then we begin to have the intelligence of God, not the intelligence of man. Understanding makes us to be skillful and wise in the Word.

3. **Criest After Knowledge:**

Proverbs 2:3
Yea if thou **criest** after knowledge, and liftest up thy voice for understanding.

Criest Hebrew) To call out, to address by name, invite, to preach, publish, that are bidden to proclaim.

We are to call and address by name, to invite the knowledge of God in our heart. We are to preach it, teach it to proclaim it, to all who will hear the Word of truth. There is a lot of Word preached throughout the country, but as we find it today it is only the flesh word (natural) the letter kills, but the spirit makes alive, what are you saying? When we give the word out of season or not by the inspiration of the Holy Ghost (anointing) you are giving the letter (law) the law brings death.

Proverbs 12:1
Whoso loveth instruction loveth knowledge: but he that hateth reproof is brutish.
Knowledge (Hebrew) skillful, make known, intelligence, sense, wise.
Understanding (Greek) insight, the faculty of comprehension.
Reproof (Hebrew) rebuke, punishment, correction, chastened, reasoning. (Greek) proof, rebuke, evidence.

When we take heed to the instruction of the Lord we will gain knowledge, we will become skillful in the Word. Book knowledge is a good thing, but without **Wisdom** it brings forth flesh (natural), it will not sustain us. We must be skillful in the Word or we become brutish.

Proverbs 9:9
Give instruction to the wise man, and he will be yet wiser; Teach a just man, and he will increase in learning.

When **Wisdom** cried out she not only went to the high places she went in to the city where the crowd was. She wanted and needed to be heard not for herself but for everyone that would hear, to come to the banquet table. She had the table ready of meat (aged word) and bread, (life) the bread was ready to be broken (Jesus' body) to eat of the Word to digest it, get it down in our bellies to be nourished so we will grow in the Grace and Knowledge of God. We are to go to the high places in God to cry out to be heard, to set at the banquet table to gather all who will hear our cry to come, eat and drink at the Master's table. How we do this? To prepare ourselves through prayer, studying, and fasting. We are to cry after knowledge, and receive instruction so we can get **Wisdom**. Not just by reading the Bible, we are to study it, rightly dividing The Word of Truth. Do not take out of context or you will err and get confused. We are to be rooted and grounded in God's unfailing love.

Proverbs 9:4
Wisdom says: who is simple let him turn in hither: as in Revelation 4:1 says-Come up hither and I will show thee things which must be here after. We are to come up to the place in God, to enter into the secret place, for he is our refuge, our High Tower, he is our hiding place.
Hither (Hebrew) to here, on this side. (Greek) come, here, in this place.

4. **Lift Up Thy Voice For Understanding:**

Proverbs 2:3
Yea, if thou cries after knowledge, and lift up thy voice for understanding.

When we lift up something, we raise it higher, or bring it to another level than it was before. We lift our voice to the Lord in skillfulness and in intelligence of God. We lift our voices in one accord in singing, with practicing; our singing becomes skillful. When we are learning a song we are not skillful we do not understand it fully, we do not understand, or know, or have **Wisdom** of the song till we learn it. But we first must listen to the song, write it down on paper, chord the song, to get the right tune to it. Then we practice the song until it is perfect, then we can sing it to the public. We are to arise and lift up our voices in The Lord we are one with him. As a choir; their voices blend in perfect harmony you cannot tell one voice apart from another, but each one different. There is the lead singer, the soprano, the low alto, the high alto, tenor, the bare-tone, base, last but not least the choir director; to direct the choir to bring in perfect harmony as there is one voice. The one voice is in perfect harmony into the worship realm, to come into one mind and one accord, it is no longer I that lives but the Christ in me. We will shine forth in the Lord, the Shekinah Glory. This is where we are caught up in the spirit (air) flesh cannot enter.

Matthew 7:7
Seek and ye shall find.

We will not find what we are looking for if we do not seek for it. When we come into the presence of the Lord we are to pray, to lift up our voice to the Lord, to lift up our hand in total surrender to sing praises unto him with our whole heart and mind, not thinking of anything around us. It is all about Him and who He is. Our sincere desire is to know him, seek Him, to praise Him in all His glory. We are to enter into His rest for He is our Rest. We cannot do this with a weak spine, we must have a backbone to stand up straight, to be bold. We must approach the Throne Room boldly. Isaiah 55:6; Seek the Lord while he may be found.

Hebrews 4:16
Let us therefore come boldly to the throne of Grace that we may obtain Mercy, and find Grace to help in the time of need.

We must stand bold! We are to stand, to be strong in the Lord in the power of His might. When we have a desire for something or someone we will not stop until we have exhausted every means we have. We will not stop until we get what we desire. Our desire is Jesus Christ, our only hope, our only way to salvation for Jesus is the door to eternal life.

Hebrews 10:19
Having therefore, brethren, **boldness** to enter into the holiest by the blood of Jesus.

We must be bold as a lion, **Boldness** to enter in by and through the blood of the Lamb.

5. ***If thou Seek Her as Silver:***

Proverbs 2:4-6
If thou seeketh her as silver, and searches for her as for hid treasures.

5th Then shalt thou understand the fear of the Lord, and find the knowledge of God.
6th For the Lord gives **Wisdom**: out of His mouth comes knowledge and understanding.
Seekest (Hebrew) To search out in worship and prayer, to strive after, desire, request a petition.

We are to seek first the Kingdom of God and all His righteousness and he will fill us. We are to seek out **Wisdom** as silver and search for the hidden treasures in God. When we are seeking we are searching, we are making our petition known unto the Lord. We make our petition known by praying the Word to God Almighty. When we make a request we are asking God to change something that needs changed in our lives. When we pray we are to know the Word, so that we can pray knowing the Word is in our heart. and pray the Word. What do you mean? How can you know the Father's will in our prayer life if we do not know the Word, how do we know we are praying amiss, or contrary to the Word of God. We are to seek until we find, we do not stop. There is no stopping place for we must continually search deeper and deeper in our walk with the Lord. We are not alone in this walk, we are a body with many membered parts, it takes the whole body fitly joined together for the Lord to have a place to lay his head upon the shoulders (strength).

St Matthew 8:20
And Jesus said unto him, the foxes have holes, and the birds of the air have nest, but the Son of Man hath not where to lay his head.

Until the body comes together and there be no more schism, to have that agape love, then will Jesus have a place to lay His head; upon our shoulders. The head and the body must come together to unite to be one to be in Him and Him in us. Right now the body is crippled, the body is slowly coming together with one Word, one song, one message, no more division! How? By seeking **Wisdom**, knowledge and understanding.

6. *Search For Her as Hidden Treasures:*

Luke 15:8
Either what woman having ten pieces of silver, if she lose one piece, doth not light a candle, and sweep the house, and seek diligently till she find it?

Hebrews 11:6
But without faith it is impossible to please him, for he comes to God must believe that He is, and that He is a rewarder of them that diligently seek Him.

Search (Hebrew) to penetrate, to examine, seek out, try. (Greek) to utter, proclaim, look into, try to find.

We must have faith, without faith we cannot be saved. Faith does not save you, but you must have the faith that God will save you. St. John 5:24; but to have faith that you have passed from death unto life. We must voice our desires to the Lord; we are to seek those things we ask for so we can open our heart to receive the promises of God. This happens a lot of times through our praise and worship, we lose ourselves when we come into the presence of God through our worship, this is where healing takes place, where prayers are answered. When we lift our hands to the Lord we are surrendering, giving the Lord complete control of our lives, our heart, mind, body and soul. This is where the enemy is confused; we are no longer giving him any power over us. This is seeking the Lord, and finding His treasures beyond measure. We are letting the Holy Ghost take control, to examine us; taking all impurities out of us. This treasure we are seeking, we will find when we seek, and knock. As we see here the woman that lost her silver (redemption) she lit, or what we call turn on a light or lamp to take out the darkness overshadowing to no longer be in darkness. She let the light shine in order to find her silver.

II Corinthians 4:6
God commanded the light to shine out of darkness, hath shined in our hearts, to give the light of the knowledge of the glory of God in face of Jesus Christ.

To command something it means to do this thing Now! God has given us commands throughout the Old Testament and the New Testament for us to do, we must do them. Search is to utter, proclaim it, look into, try to find the treasures. When we search we examine every corner, nook and cranny, nothing left unturned. We go into a room full of darkness we can't see, nevertheless try to find something. First we must turn on the light to push out the darkness, then we began to look, this is what takes place when we let God in our lives and he turns on the light in us, no longer in darkness, we found our Silver (redemption) we found our treasure. For Jesus Christ is the light, that shines forth out of darkness.

Isaiah 40:31
They that wait upon the Lord shall renew their strength: they shall mount up with wings as eagles; they shall run and not be weary; and they shall walk and not faint.

Wing (Hebrew) corner, hem (hem) skirt, border, uttermost part, ends of the earth.

The eagle as we all know is the king of all birds. The eagle flies above the clouds, above the beggarly elements. The eagle has strength in his wings to fly above all birds. We are like an eagle, to soar above all situations of life. It has been said that the eagle can see as far as a hundred miles away, and capable of picking up a lot of weight. So when we wait on the Lord and He renews our strength we will run with patience, we will walk the walk of faith, if we faint not.

John 5:39
He says search the scriptures; for in them you think you have eternal life; and they are they which testify of me.

There was a time in my life I thought I was alright; only to find out I was not alright. I was in bondage of the traditions of men. As I grew in the Lord, prayed and studied His Word I began to grow. I prayed with a sincere heart for the Lord to teach me, to remove all things I had been taught of men's traditions and teach me. We are to seek God and His ways, not man's ways.

Ecclesiastes 1:13
And I gave my heart to *SEEK* and *SEARCH* out by **Wisdom** concerning all things that are done under heaven.

We the people have erred by listening totally to men, not getting in the Bible to study for ourselves. I am not downing preachers, teacher, pastors and evangelists, prophets or apostles. I am saying we rely too much on our Pastors, teachers, and evangelists more than we rely on God. We are human and we must study and read for ourselves. We must pray and study. Get alone with God, nobody else can do that for us. We must seek God for ourselves. We are to seek God and His way not man's way.

7. ***Then Thou Shalt Understand the Fear of The Lord:***

Proverbs 1:7
The *fear* of the Lord is the beginning of **Knowledge**, but fools despise **Wisdom** and instruction.
Then thou shalt understand the *fear* of the Lord and find instruction, to be taught, to make known the deep things of God. We need to recognize and see the fear or awesomeness of our Lord and Savior.
Knowledge (Hebrew) Seeing, recognize, instruction, acknowledge, to make known, teach, be learned.

Proverbs 3:13
Happy is the man that finds **Wisdom** and the man that gets understanding. Lord preserve *knowledge*, and he that overthrows the words of a transgressor.

When we find **Wisdom** we find a good thing. **Wisdom** brings reverence unto the Lord, brings knowledge and knowledge brings understanding, which is a wellspring of life springing up within us. **Wisdom** causes us to hear the instructions of the Lord, to be teachable so that we can learn, to acknowledge the Word of the Lord.

II Timothy 3:16
All scripture is given by inspiration of God, and is profitable for doctrine, for reproof, for correction, for instruction in righteousness.

Isaiah 47:10
For thou has trusted in thy wickedness: thou hast said, none sees me. Thy **Wisdom** and thy knowledge, it hast perverted thee; and thou hath said in thine heart, I am and none else beside me.

There is only **_One I Am!_**

Exodus 3:14
Moses asked God what do I do I say unto them?
14th verse; ***I Am The I Am!***

We are not to lean to our own understanding, nor can we cannot look at what we have done. We have done nothing. The Lord does the work through us, we are a vessel he works through. We are to look to the Lord for our help, for our help comes from the Lord. We are never to look at ourselves and say "Look what I have done!" We just lifted up self and not God. We are giving ourselves glory not God. We must be careful or we will use God's name in vain, for our self-glory. People think when we use God's name in vain we are saying a bad word. We are just asking God to Destroy something, we use God for our glory we are taking his name in vain. It is what the Lord has done, not us.

Full of the Holy Ghost and Wisdom:

Acts 6:3
Wherefore brethren, look ye among you, seven men of honest report, full of the Holy Ghost and **Wisdom**, whom we may appoint over this business.

The apostles stated the stipulation is that the seven men are to be full of the Holy Ghost. They cannot do the business of the church without the fullness of the Holy Ghost.
1. Of honest report
2. Full of the Holy Ghost
3. Full of **Wisdom**

Matthew 3:11
Acts 2:3 & Acts 1:8 power for witnessing to the people

The Terms of the Holy Ghost:
1. The Baptism of the Holy Ghost
2. Filled with the Holy Ghost Acts 4:8 & 13:9
3. Gifts of the Holy Ghost.

Proverbs 9
The *fear* of the Lord is the beginning of **Wisdom**: and knowledge of the Holy is understanding.

What is the *fear* of the Lord?
1. To hate evil: All things that are contrary to the Word of God
2. To hate all arrogance: Full of pride and haughty 1 Timothy 3:6;
3. To hate all evil ways: Wicked, trouble, adversity, anything that does not pertain to God.
4. To hate forward mouth: not easily controlled; willful; contrary.

Deuteronomy 10:12
And now all Israel, what does the Lord thy God require of thee, but to **FEAR** (reverence) the Lord thy God, to walk in

all His ways, and to love him, and to serve the Lord thy God with ALL thy heart with all thy soul.

To fear the Lord is not to be scared to death of Him like a wicked father would beat his son half to death. To fear the Lord is to reverence Him, to love Him, to honor and adore Him to serve him whole heartedly. We are not to lean unto our own understanding; but to lean on the Lord's understanding. When we reverence Him we love him, serve him, this is the beginning of **Wisdom**.

Proverbs 24:5
A Wise man is strong; yea a man of knowledge increased in strength.

The Lord wants us to be bold and to be strong. The way to be strong is to have the fear of the Lord, (awe and reverence) to walk in His ways to put Him first, to have Him Lord of our homes, our finances, our children in all points of our lives.

Proverbs 24:14
So shall the knowledge of **Wisdom** be unto thy soul; when thou hast found it, then there shall be a reward, and thy expectation shall be cut off.
In other words we shall enter into His treasures and find eternal life. We must have the mind of Christ. To know His way, to know his Word, for the Truth will make us free.

Philippians 2:5
Let this mind be ***IN YOU!*** Which is also in Jesus Christ.

The mind of Christ is to have the anointing and the power of the Holy Ghost, so we may enter into the joys of the Lord. Let us go back to the (Hebrew) meaning once again. **Knowledge** means to teach, instruct, prosper, and to guide, to come fully acquainted with, to acknowledge. We are to teach a wise man and he will become wiser. We are to set aside the young ministers. We are to teach them on how to study the bible and to show them the whole salvation plan so that they might see and know their callings and elections.

When we are guided by the spirit we will ascend to higher levels of learning, there is no stopping place here when it comes to learning. We are always studying, learning the Word.

I Kings 4:29
And God gave Solomon **Wisdom** and understanding exceeding much, and largeness of heart, even as the sand that is on the sea shore. Solomon wanted **Wisdom** and knowledge so that he also can help the people that came before him.

Now I say he was not thinking of himself (not Selfish) he was thinking how he could help his people. To put his people first, Solomon had a heart of God.

Job 11:6
And that he would shew thee the secrets of **Wisdom**, that they are double to that which is! Know thereof that God exacteth thee less than thine iniquity deserves.

The secrets here are double, the measure twice as much as normal **Wisdom**,
7th Canst thou by searching find out God: can't thou find out the Almighty God unto perfection?

Matthew 5:48
Be ye therefore perfect, (mature) even as your Father which is in heaven perfect.

Our flesh cannot ever be perfected, but the spirit man is the one that has to put on perfection. Jesus Christ has taken His abode in us the day we were born again. He is burning all the impurities or the dross out of us. This place we are in is hot and it is an uncomfortable place, for it burns out the bonds of traditions. We are to walk through, the desert places and deep dark valleys. The valleys are for learning and burning. God is a consuming fire and God took his abode in us the day we were born again.

Malachi 3:2
Who may abide in the day of His coming? And who shall stand when he appears? For he is like a refiner's fire, and fuller's soap.

This is not talking about the last days when he comes again, he is talking of when we come to him we are born again, began at the house of God (within us) the cleansing fires are on, He is speaking of the Fuller's soap. He is washing us clean and pure, washing us through His Word. Can we stand the fire? We are in the refinery, we are the clay he is molding, shaping us as he is molding and shaping us he has water (Word) flowing through us. Then we are taken off the potter's wheel, we are put in the oven for firing; the fires are hot and it is bringing us through, then when we are taken out of the fire there is a glaze to paint on the vessel then back into the fires, great cleansings are on. A precious vessel comes forth, a vessel of honor, as gold tried in the fires.

Romans 9:21
Hath not the potter power over the clay, of the same lump to make one vessel of honor and to another dishonor.

Fuller's Soap (Hebrew) to wash, launder, to be washed, washer.
Fire (Greek) to purify

Hebrews 12:29
For God is a consuming fire.

Jeremiah 20:9
But his word was in mine heart as a burning fire shut up in my bones, and I was weary with forbearing; and I could not stay.

As I said earlier, perfection is growing and maturing in the Lord, Knowing His Word. The more we study the more we pray the more the old man dies out and the more that the spirit man lives. There is a war going on inside of us the war of good and evil. Our spirit is willing but our flesh is weak.

Hebrews 12:23
To the general assembly and the church of the firstborn, which are written in heaven, and to God the judge of all, and to the spirits of just men made ***perfect.***

We are in Christ, Christ in us so the Christ in us made perfect (Mature) so we can be perfect.

St. John 3:30
John said this: He must increase, but I must decrease.

The more of God we know the less flesh will arise. We are to squeeze the life out of the old man Adam by maturing and growing up into **Wisdom**. We need **Wisdom** and knowledge, which come from the Father that will sustain us in our natural lives such as careers, work, home, and children. This **Wisdom** from above is peaceable, pure, it will sustain you. Remember **Wisdom** was before the world was created, before the mountains the oceans so forth. Such great **Wisdom** to be there to see these things brought forth.

Job 12:12
With the Ancient is *Wisdom*; and in the length of days understanding.

Proverbs 18:4
The words of a man's mouth are as deep waters, and the wellspring of *Wisdom* as a flowing brook.

Proverbs 16:22
Understanding is a wellspring of life unto him that hath it; but the instruction of fools is folly.
There is a wellspring of *Wisdom* as well as a wellspring of life. These must flow through us freely. Our mouth is to have a continuing flowing of the Word. To speak the Words of life and to bring forth life, springing up within our spirit man.
St. John 4:14
But whosoever drinks of the water that I give him shall never thirst; but the water that I give him shall be IN him a well of water springing up into everlasting life.

Psalms 136:5
To him that *Wisdom* made the heavens: for his mercy endures forever.

Genesis 1:1
In the beginning God created the heaven and the earth.

You see there is a change took place. From the first verse to the second verse; God is separating everything putting everything back in order. When he created the heaven and the earth God spoke it into existence. What he made he made everything good it was beautifully and wonderfully made. Whether we think twenty-four hour days or what, a day with the Lord is a thousand years or a thousand years as one day. Time did not start until man fell, so we do not know how long Adam was in the Garden of Eden till he fell. He could have been there a billion years. I do not believe the minute Eve was brought forth she went right to the tree of good and evil and sinned.

Genesis 1:2
And the earth was without form, and void; and darkness was upon the face of the deep. And the spirit moved upon the face of the deep.

This is the letter, the natural (Logos word), let me bring in some balance here; the (Rhema spirit) where the spirit makes alive.

When we were yet sinners we were in darkness, we had no form, we were empty (void). Then we came to the Lord we were born again, We let His light shine in us, no longer in darkness, we took on His form no longer empty, and the spirit took up residence making us alive. He gave us His power, His name, praise the Lord this is life here!

Hosea 4:6
My people are destroyed for the lack of knowledge.

Why? They reject the truth; they want what their denomination wants. Their pastor preaches it they believe it without going to their Bibles to see for themselves. They want on the band wagon of acceptance. I had a woman tell me that is not what (I won't say her denomination) my church teaches.

Even though I had shown her in the Bible it did not matter. What I am saying here is; Study right along with the Pastor, or whoever is ministering at that time, do not take for granted. We are never to rely on someone for our salvation or never put a pastor up to the point we worship the pastor instead of the Lord, and unfortunately it happens. We are to reverence our pastor (he is our shepherd or leader) and our leaders but never worship or put ahead of God, if we do we have committed spiritual adultery, this is anyone we put before God.

Exodus 20:3
Thou shalt have no other gods before me.
14th thou shalt not commit adultery.
There is spiritual adultery, Let us go to Prophet Hosea.

Hosea 9:1
Rejoice NOT! O Israel, for joy, as other people, for thou hast gone a whoring from thy God, thou hast loved a reward upon every corn floor.

This is harsh words, but the truth will make you free. When we lack knowledge we are bringing damnation to our soul, we are speaking death not life. We will enter into the enemies trap if we are not careful. As we grow up in the Lord we will gain **Wisdom.** We must grow or we stunt our growth, we be like a child, immature.

I Corinthians 13:11
When I was a child, I spake as child, I understood as a child, I thought as a child: but when I become a man I put away childish things.

Paul said; we are to grow up in the Lord; it is a constant learning and growing. We are to understand, to think or act as a grown man would, as we mature. We began to lose interest in our games we play, such as trucks and cars; playhouse cribs and dolls, these toys they are only make believe; symbolic to real life. We no longer think the same or act the way as we did when we were young. When we grow up into maturity we began to lay our toys down, we are no longer playing games; we are in reality. We grow up in the admiration of the Holy Ghost.

Ephesians 3:19
And to know the love of Christ, which passes knowledge, that ye might be filled with all the fullness of God.

We can only know the love of God when we come into the family of God to be born again in the newness of life. We are changed no longer the same. We grow daily by the washing of the Word to eat daily of His bread for it becomes life to the soul.

Job 11:6-7
The secrets of **Wisdom** is double.

7th Canst thou be searching find out the Almighty unto perfection.

The secret to **Wisdom** is to know the Lord and His way. Worldly **Wisdom** differs from heavenly **Wisdom**, this **Wisdom** from above is double the secret of this **Wisdom** is to know the Lord God Almighty.

Notes

Chapter 3

How to Gain and Keep Wisdom

Job 28:28
And unto man he said, behold the fear of the Lord that is **Wisdom**: and to depart from evil is understanding.

Fear: reverence, Piety, dreadful, exceedingly afraid. (Greek) To fear, be afraid, alarmed, an impediment to faith and love; to reverence, respect, worship, a proper fear for God, a deep reverence and awe dreadful terrible.
Piety (Greek) godliness, piety, holiness, to worship,

The fear of the Lord is: Reverence to be in awe of Him. To look to Him in admiration.

James 4:17
Therefore to him that knows to do good, and doeth it not, to him it is a sin.

Psalms 86:11
Teach my thy way oh Lord, I will walk I thy truth; unite my heart to fear thy name.

So our hearts desire should be to walk in thy truth to have our hearts coupled in the fear of the Lord, and to walk in His statues (portion, ordinances).

Ezekiel 44:24
And in controversy shall they stand in: and they shall judge it according to my s: and they shall keep my laws and statues (ordinances) all mine assemblies and they shall hallow (make hollow) Sabbaths.

Psalms 112:1-6
Praise the Lord, blessed is the man that fears the Lord that delights greatly in his commandments.
2nd His seed shall be mighty on the earth; the generation of the upright shall be blessed
3rd Wealth and riches shall be in his house: and his righteousness endures forever.
4th Unto the upright there arises light in the darkness: he is gracious, full of compassion and righteousness.
5th A good man shows favor, and lendeth; will guide his affairs with discretion.
6th Surely he shall not be moved forever; the righteousness shall be in everlasting remembrance.

The Gift of Wisdom

I Corinthians 12:4-11
Now there are diversities (different) of gifts, but the same spirit. 8th for to one I given by the spirit the WORD of **Wisdom**, to another he Word of **Knowledge** by the same spirit.

Spiritual gifts are not given on basis of merits or on good behavior, or they are better than the other, it is given to each person as Christ places them in the body to profit all and according to God's will and plan. True **Wisdom** of God is perfect, not in **Wisdom** of this world as man sees it to be. Our faith should not stand in the **Wisdom** of man but in the power of the Holy Ghost. The gifts did not die out with the Apostles; they are still alive and very active. If the gifts died out with the apostles then the church lost its ability to operate in the Holy Ghost, for it has no **Wisdom**, knowledge or understanding.

Manifold Wisdom:

Ephesians 3:10
To the intent that now unto the principalities and powers in heavenly places might be known by the church the manifold **Wisdom** of God.

Manifold **Wisdom** (Hebrew) Abundant, increase, multiply. (Greek) various, diverse.

They behold the astonishing ***Wisdom*** of God as he demonstrates the **Wisdom** through the church. Not in worldly **Wisdom** but Godly ***Wisdom***.

II Corinthians 2:17
For we are not as many, which corrupt the Word of God: but as of sincerity, but as of God, in the sight of God speak we in Christ.

There is a difference in God's ***Wisdom*** and in the Worldly **Wisdom**, God's **Wisdom** brings life unto the soul and it is joy unspeakable. Worldly **Wisdom** brings death and damnation to our soul, it profits nothings.

James 1:5-6
If any lacks **Wisdom**, let him ask of God that gives all to men liberally, and unbraided not; and it shall be given him.

6th but let him ask in faith nothing wavering. For he that wavers is like a wave of sea driven with the wind and tossed.

We are to ask in faith believing not doubting nothing wavering (swaying). He will give to you liberally, not to be in need. But first we have to ask in sincerity in the word or deed. We are to ask with our whole heart, believing he will give us our hearts desire, only if it is based on the Word of God.

I Corinthians 2:7
But we speak the *Wisdom* of God in a mystery, even the hidden *Wisdom* which God ordained before the world unto our glory.

Mystery (Greek) secret, unveiled, often misunderstood part of the Old Testament

The only way to uncover the mystery is to know the Old Testament; to uncover the truth of the Tabernacle of Moses. The cross is hidden within in the Tabernacle, unveiled in the New Testament in Jesus Christ. This hidden Truth, this mystery, this secret is; knowing the full salvation plan. We only know in parts. The salvation plan is revealed in the first fifteen chapters of Acts. It is not just repenting this is just only going through the gate to the brazen alter to give a blood sacrifice; Repentance and baptism of water, which is symbolic of death burial and resurrection according to Romans 6:3-6; the thirty fold Christian. They are three steps to the salvation plan; the tabernacle is the pattern of salvation there is the gate, to the Outer Courts, Repentance; The Door, Holy of Holies, filled with the Holy Ghost; which is Pentecost; the baptism of the Holy Ghost, the 60 fold Christian. Then there is the 100 fold Christian the tabernacles, which the veil is rent, the veil is lifted off our eyes, which very few has entered, this is for the mature, or perfect Christian where it is no longer I but Christ in me.

I Corinthians 2:9-10
But it Is written, eye hath not seen, nor ears heard, neither have entered into the heart of man, the things which God hath prepared for them that love him.
10th but God **HATH REVEALED** them to us by His **SPIRIT!** For the spirit searches all things, yea *the deep things of God.*

We always heard the 9th verse, but nobody goes unto the next verse; God is revealing to us His Word. He is revealing them to us by His spirit. He is opening up the mystery through the Old Testament there is no way you can understand the fullness until you know the Tabernacle of Moses and the life of Moses being the pattern Son!

Revelation 21:2-3
And I John saw that Holy City, **New Jerusalem, coming down from God out of Heaven,** prepared as a bride adorned for her husband.
3rd And I heard a great voice out of heaven saying, behold, the tabernacle of God is with men, and he will dwell with them, and they shall be his people, and **God Himself shall be with them and be their God.**

Our body is the earth, and the head (Christ) the heaven. I know this seems off the wall, but if you go to Corinthians and study out the body of Christ it says he is the head of the body. So if he is the Head (heaven) and we are His body (earth) so the heavens and the earth have got to come together.

I Corinthians 12: 1-31
I am not going to write all the whole chapter of Corinthians down it would be too much. But please go to it and study it all out. Run references on this chapter, get a concordance to look up the meanings of the words.

I Peter 1:10-12
Of which salvation the prophets have enquired and searched diligently, who prophesied of grace that should come to unto you.

Ephesians 2:8-9
For by Grace ye are saved through faith, and that not of yourselves, it is the gift of God;
9th not of works, lest any man boasts.

We, as men cannot save ourselves; it is by and through the blood of Christ that he shed on Calvary. Salvation is a gift, given to every man that will accept this gift. Our works cannot and will not save us. We can use every gift and calling he has given us, but we must first be saved through the blood of Jesus Christ. Or our works are in vain. We are all born with a gift or gifts in our lives, we can use them but they are unprofitable without Grace.

Ephesians 2:19-20
For by Grace ye are saved through faith; and not of yourselves, it is the gift of God;
9th not of works, lest any man should boast.

The scripture here speaks of the Gentiles being grafted in. The Jews being God's chosen people, the Gentiles being same or no different than a dog, but by the shedding of Jesus' precious blood was poured out for all mankind. We are in the dispensation of Grace where every man can be saved regardless of what race he is. I like the song that a sister in the Lord wrote: (Charlotte Torango) God is building a house where creation shall dwell. The house he is building is with you and with me. With Jesus the Chief Corner Stone.

Matthew 14:1-3
Let not your heart be troubled, ye believe in God, believe also in me.
2nd In my Father's house are many **_MANSIONS_**: if it were not so, I would have told you so, I go to prepare a place for you.

This is what happened on the Day of Pentecost, His spirit was poured out on everyone, regardless of race color or creed. We are His mansions he is building, He being the Chief Corner Stone. It is not a natural mansion as we have here on earth. These mansions are with you and with me. Jesus took His abode in us the day we were born again. He is perfecting each one of us. He is building His Kingdom with each of us coming together no more twain (two) but ONE (unity) NEW MAN, Jesus being the HEAD. We do not serve a far off God way beyond the blue, He is within us. He took his abode within us the day we asked Him into our heart. Jesus said if you abide in me, I abide in you; we come one with Jesus.

St. John 14:20
At that day ye shall know that I am in my Father, and ye in me, and I in you.

We are to become one with Jesus, as Jesus, as Jesus is one with the Father, to come inseparable no longer twain (two).

Wisdom Builds Her House On Seven Pillars

When we come to the Lord, our ground (earth, Adam flesh) nature is broken, Jesus being the Chief Corner Stone. We have to have a solid foundation which Jesus is the Solid Rock of our Salvation. Then up comes the wall which protect us from the enemy, it keeps out the enemy, it keeps out danger from us. This represents our bodies; we put on the roof to be covered. Jesus is our covering from the storms of life. The windows when they are installed in our house then He will open up the windows of heaven and pour out blessings we cannot contain, I am talking about our spiritual house. Then the electric in installed for lighting, a light that cannot be hid that we be not in darkness. Jesus is our light and we are the light of the world. Then the water pipes must be installed for us to have flowing water freely as we need, the water representing the spirit and it must flow freely. Then we hang the door; Jesus is the door we must enter in through the door. We are not to climb up any other way.

Isaiah 60:1
Arise shine; for the light is come, and the glory of the Lord is risen upon thee.

Hebrews 9:11
But Christ being come an high priest of good things to come, by a greater and more perfect tabernacle, not made with hands, that is to say, not of this building.

Romans 8:18-19
For I reckon that the suffering of this **PRESENT TIME** are not worthy to be compared with the glory which shall be **<u>REVEALED IN US!</u>**
Read this very carefully! It does **NOT SAY REVEALED TO US; It SAYS IN US!** We are longing in our spirit and waiting for the

time we see the manifestation of the Sons to come together, it is happening now. It is a process, but it is happening.

You are wondering; what has this got to do with attaining **Wisdom**? We are to possess to recover the **Wisdom** and to have a balance of the whole, the Bible.

Notes

Chapter 4

What is the Fear of the Lord?

What is the Fear of the Lord!

Proverbs 8:13
The fear of the Lord is to hate evil, pride, and arrogancy, and the evil way, and the forward mouth do I hate.

1. Hate Evil:

   We are not only hate evil, we are to shun it. We are not to be on the edge and flirt with sin, you are temping the Lord thy God, your heart is not fully persuaded to fully serve the true and living God. **Hate** (Hebrew) enemy, foe (Greek) to detest.

   Isaiah 13:11
   And I will punish the world for their evil, and I will cause the arrogancy of the proud to cease, and will lay low the haughtiness of the terrible.

   Titus 2:12
   Teaching us that, denying ungodliness and worldly lusts, we should live soberly, righteously, and godly, in this present world.

2. **Hate Pride**:

Proverbs 16:18-19
Pride goes before destruction, and a haughty spirit before a fall.
19th Better it is to be of an humble spirit with the lowly, than to divide the spoil with the proud.

3. **Hate Arrogancy**:

Arrogancy (Hebrew) Pride, proud, haughtiness.

Jeremiah 48:29
We have heard the pride of Mo'ab, (he is exceeding proud) his loftiness, and his arrogancy, and his pride, and the haughtiness of his heart.

4. **Hate Evil Ways**:

Job 1:1
There was a man in the land of Uz, whose name was Job; and that man was perfect (mature) and upright, (righteous) and one that feared God (reverend and in awe), and eschewed evil (to depart from).

We are not only to hate evil, we are to stay away from the evil, trouble or adversity, anything that does not pertain to God. We must live a holy life; we are not to desire the world and its evil strategies.
Eschewed (Hebrew) Turned-off, decline depart, to reject, decline.

Zechariah 8:17
And let none of you imagine evil in your hearts against his neighbor; love no false oath: for all these things that I hate, said the Lord.

5. **Hate A Froward Mouth**:

A forward mouth is not easily controlled. He sows strife and whispers gossip and he brings separation wherever he goes. It only takes the Holy Ghost to bridle the tongue.

Froward (Hebrew) crooked, warped, perverse (Greek) corrupt, crooked, untoward.

Proverbs 3:32
For the forward is an abomination to the Lord: but his secret is with the righteous.

I know I gave this in chapter two: How do you pursue **Wisdom**? I need to bring it out another way along with chapter four: What is the fear of the Lord? It is interchangeable, it goes with both chapters. This is a great study and I believe it is necessary to overlap in certain areas.

Hebrews 12:8-9
But ye be without chastisement, whereof all partakers, then ye are bastards, (illegitimate) and not sons.
9th Furthermore we have had fathers of our flesh which corrected us, and we gave them reverence; shall we not much rather be in subjection unto our heavenly Father above and live?

Whew! These are harsh words here; but true. In times past when a child was born out of wedlock the child could not take their father's name, for they were not married so they had to take the mother's maiden name which meant they had no father, for it meant they had no surname. The child was labeled an illegitimate child.

We have a heavenly Father who chastises us, his children, or he corrects us. We are to incline our ears to listen to his correction and acknowledge him as our heavenly Father. We must take his correction or we are the same as no father, and we are spiritually become an illegitimate child. I did not say this, the Bible said it.

Proverbs 15:32-33
He that refuses instruction despises his own soul: but he that hears reproof gets **understanding.**
33rd *The Fear of the Lord* is instruction of **Wisdom**: and before honor is humility.
Reproof (Hebrew) Chastisement, proof, correction, rebuke. (Greek) Conviction, proof, rebuke.

We cannot afford to refuse the Lord's instruction or reject his voice. We are his children growing up into sons; we are to listen as a son listens to his father's lecture. Sometimes we did not like it; but as children it made us grow into maturity. When we hear the instructions of our heavenly Father we hear his correction, conviction, and feel his chastisement through the Holy Ghost which brings us into humility maturity, and understanding. We are not to despise his instruction or we bring hate into our hearts for ourselves. We are to bring honor unto the Lord when we do we bring honor unto ourselves.

Isaiah 53:5
But he was wounded for our transgressions, he was bruised for our iniquities: the chastisement of our peace was upon him and with his stripes we are healed.
Transgression (Hebrew) trespass, our sin, (Greek) violation
Iniquities (Hebrew) Fault, evil, mischief, (Greek) unrighteous, wickedness.

He was wounded for our trespasses, our sins, and violations, he was bruised for our evil ways, our mischief, our unrighteousness, and our wickedness; our correction of our peace was upon him. He came to redeem it all back at Calvary. He took the stripes on his back for our healing, but most of all the main sickness was sin sickness.
Bruised (Hebrew) To be contrite, to crush, break in pieces, humbled, oppress, smitten down.

Proverbs 16:16-17
How much better is it to get *Wisdom* than gold! And to get *understanding* rather to be chosen as silver.
17th The highway of the upright is to depart from evil: he that keeps his way preserves his soul.

When we get the Heavenly **Wisdom** we are far richer than any earthly gold. Understanding in our walk with the Lord is far better than chosen silver. We are to depart from man's evil ways such as pride, a haughty spirit, an evil tongue, forwardness and a lying tongue. We are to be of a humble spirit with a wellspring of life springing up within us flowing out of our mouths.

Proverbs 19:20-23
Hear wise counsel, and receive instruction, and thou may be wise in the latter end.

21st There are many devises in a man's heart; nevertheless the counsel of the Lord shall stand.

We must hear (incline) our ears unto wise counsel, which is **Wisdom**, which gives instructions that we will be able to stand. A man has many devises deep in his heart and mind, they may be good they may evil, but regardless of the situation The Word of the Lord will prevail.

I John 1:27
But whoso hath this World's good, and sees his brother have need, and shut up his bowels of compassion from him, how dwelleth the love of God in him.
Bowels (Greek) the spleen; an intense, pity or sympathy, inward affection

If we have not sympathy or enough love in us to have tender mercy as our heavenly Father has for his children then we do not have the love of God. When we do not have the love of God in our heart's we cannot show love. It is not in the natural man to show this kind of love, our flesh man Adam has a selfish love, it is all about him and if it does not profit him he has no desire for it or any part of it. Man's natural tendencies are selfish, unaffectionate, unmerciful, has no sympathy other than himself. The natural man will give money, food and clothes to organizations to the needy if it profit him such as a tax write off, or to be noticed, so people will be whispering did you see what he or she gave, did you hear about Mr. So and So he gave this amount, just to be recognized. Such as the Sadducee's and Pharisee's they did much praying in places just to be seen. They gave much money trying to out give one another, just to be recognized. This is how we all are, it is in all of us, if we would only stand back and take a look at ourselves. When we recognize who we are without the Lord and that we are in lack of love then we can surrender all to God, when we do we give in secret, we pray in secret, then God will reward us openly.

Psalms 133:1
Behold, (look) how good and pleasant is it for the brethren to dwell in unity.

It only takes the Holy Ghost dwelling in our house (hearts) for us to be able to dwell in unity, or in one accord. When the spirit takes over it shuts our mouth, it opens our eyes, and our ears to the true and living God. For us to come into one mind and in one accord to dwell in unity, that God is showing us how to walk in. How do you think this took place? On the Day of Pentecost! They had come into **_One Place, One Accord, One Mind, One Voice!_** This took place by getting down to serious praying, fasting, forgetting everything around them. This did not come in one hour or one day it took ten days of tarrying to get in unity, the **HOLY GHOST** came as mighty rushing wind (spirit) and **Filled** the place where they were.

I Corinthians 1:10
Now I beseech you, brethren, by the name of our Lord Jesus Christ, that ye all speak the same thing, and that there be no divisions among you; but that ye be perfectly joined together in the same mind in the same
Joined (Greek) to restore, put in order, to mend, to make complete, equip, to prepare
(Greek) purpose, consent, advise, agree, will
Divisions (Greek) split, discord, schism, rent, tear, damage to the unity of the original group, broken

We are not to have any divisions among us, in other words no discord to damage the body of Christ. When they are discord among the brethren it brings splits in the churches, it wounds people's hearts, it tears down, breaks people into pieces that takes God to mend. Then the leaders have no compassion to restore the person or to take this matter into prayer they say in their heart oh well they deserved it, but let the shoes be on their foot, they will see with a different light. I heard people say well I can give a righteous judgment, and condemn them. The call is to agree in unity they need prayer not condemnation. To look through the EYE of God and see their need is Jesus, that's the righteous judgment. The **FEAR** of the Lord is: Reverence, to honor the Lord, when we cast out our brethren and do not try to restore them; then where is the **_Fear_** of the Lord? Think about this, we are not honoring the Lord; we are coming against one of his children so how can we honor the Lord, and have reverence of him when we hurt our Lord?

Colossians 9:10
Lie not to one another; seeing that ye have put off the **old man** with his deeds;
10th And have not put on the **new man**, which is renewed in knowledge after the image of him that created him.

Ephesians 4:4-24
There is **one body, one spirit**, even as ye are called in one hope of your calling;
8th Wherefore he said, when he ascended up on high, he led captivity captive, and gave gift unto men.
13th Till we come in the unity of the faith, and of the knowledge of the son of God, unto **A perfect man,**
unto the measure of the stature of the **fullness of Christ.**

14th That we henceforth be no more children tossed to and fro, and carried about with every wind of doctrine, by the sleight of men, and cunning craftiness, whereby they lie in wait to deceive.
16th From whom the whole body fitly joined together and compacted by that which every joint supplies, according to the effectual working in the measure of every part, makes increase of the body unto edifying itself in love.
22nd That putting off concerning the former conversation the old man, which is corrupt according to the deceitful lusts.
23rd And be renewed in the spirit of your mind.
24th And that ye put on the new man, which after God is created in righteousness and true holiness.
Cunning (Greek) deception, craftiness,
Craftiness (Greek) deception, cunning,
Effectual (Greek) working, energy, strong, shew forth, fervent.
Stature (Greek) life, life in time, age, height

The first Adam (flesh) we all die, But the Second Adam we are all made to live. The first Adam was earthy made from the ground; the second Adam is from above and pure. He supplies, every joint it's measure. He gives us life eternal and the first Adam gives us death and everything that gets in his path is destruction. We are no longer tossed about with every wind and doctrine, no longer in deception we are strong and mighty in the Lord. We come to the full age, grown in full height of the Lord. To know the Word for the Word we know makes us free. We must know the Word, not of the Word or it will not make us free. This word puts us in the true body of Christ, fitly joined as the Lord sees fit. This body is renewed daily through the Word, and through prayer. This new body or new man is created in righteousness and true holiness. True holiness is having a desire for the Lord and his way and to lift up, (not condemn), to give the Word in love, to love your brother through the love of God. To look through the

EYE (singular) God for he is full of light, not looking through your eyes for they are double and in darkness. When we put on Christ and Him crucified and we have the love in us; the love is in us because we love the brethren. Nowhere in the Bible are we to but down, condemn, destroy, when we preach the Word the Word will set mankind free. This is True **Wisdom** from above.

Daniel 3:13-17
When King Neb-u-chad-nezzar was raged and his furry commanded to bring Shadrach, Meshach, and Abed-ne-go, then they brought these men before the King.
14th Neb-u-chad-nezzer spake unto them, is it true, O Shadrach, Meshach, and Abed-ne-go, do you not serve my god's or worship the golden image which I have set up?
16th Shadrach, Meshach, and Abed-ne-go answered and said to the King, O Neb-u-chad-nezzar, If it be so, our God whom we serve is able to deliver us out of thine hand, O King.

Read all of chapter three in Daniel if you would. You will see the whole picture. We have heard so much throughout our lifetime how God delivered these three Hebrew Boys. There is a spiritual lesson here as well. We are bound with traditions of men, we have been taught things in error. We are thrown into the furnace fires of afflictions (not sickness) to burn off all the dross. We are thrown in the fire to come through the fires not delivered from the fires. There have been many times that we have had to make so many hard choices and to weigh the matter out, not knowing what to do. Then a scripture comes to mind, or someone comes by to give us a word, we know we must stand on it by faith. You might be wondering what does this have to do with **Wisdom, Knowledge and Understanding**. It has a lot to do with it. If the Hebrew boys looked at their own **Wisdom** and knowledge and leaned to their own understanding, they would have said, "I do not want to die". The Lord would understand that I was forced to worship the idols, the golden image; I had no choice in the matter. They would have thrown me in the furnace and I would have died." They would not have faced death, but they would have died a spiritual death, this is the true **Wisdom**. They used their Godly **Wisdom and Knowledge**; to lean to God's **Understanding**. In our spiritual walk with the Lord we come to the crossroads of life, they are decisions to make; for we do not like to leave the comfort zone. We also do not like to leave the bandwagon of being accepted, we like to be noticed; to feel loved and do not want to be rejected. This is the time to realize God is calling out the ones who will hear what the spirit is saying to your church to come out of bondage of the traditions of men and to worship Him in spirit and in truth. When we are bound up in bonds of traditions and we are thrown in the furnace fire of afflictions the Lord is there with us. God is a consuming fire burning up the dross in us. He is burning of the bonds of traditions in us. We come through the refinery fires, burning off the bondage of sin; and we will rise up as with eagle wings high above all birds, above the clouds to soar above all circumstances of life's trials. We will no longer be bound, we will rise up a brand new man; this is the Fear of the Lord. When you come out of the furnace fires you will come out as gold is tried in the fires, you will be a vessel of honor that has been molded on the potter's wheel then placed in the fire to hold the mold to be firm then the second firing is where you come out shining and a finished product.

Let's go back Genesis. When God told Noah to build and ark and men began to multiply on the face of the earth. Men's thought were continually evil and it repented the Lord that He had made man and grieved him at his heart. Genesis 6:1-6.

Genesis 6:8-12
But Noah found grace in the eyes of the Lord.
9th These are the generations of Noah: Noah was a just man and perfect in his generations, and Noah walked with God.
12th And God looked upon the earth, and behold, it was corrupt; for all flesh had corrupted his way upon the earth.

God told Noah to build the ark of gopher wood: (acacia wood thought to be water proof). Not only did he tell him to build the ark, he gave him instructions how to build the ark. God told him what kind of wood, how long and how wide how high to build the ark. In today's language it would be called the blueprints, they had to be drawn up before you could build.

Genesis 6:15-16
And this is the fashion which thou shall make of it; the length of the ark to be three hundred cubits, (300 complete, divine, deliverance). The breadth of it fifty cubits (anointing, jubilee, Pentecost). Height of it thirty cubits (full stature, Jesus started his ministry, the blood of Christ)
16th A window shall thou make to the ark, and in a cubit shall finish it above; and third stories thou shall make it.

The first story; one means unity, second story; two means division, union, witness of man, third story; three means divine completeness, resurrection power and life same as seven and balance. The door on the side represents Jesus being the door, when He was on the cross they pierced His side (rib), blood and water flowed. This represents the birth of the church.
Cubit (Hebrew) A measure of the forearm (**below the elbow**). Approximately 18/21 inches from the index finger to the elbow.

Genesis 6:18
But with thee will I establish my covenant; and thou shall come into the ark, thou and thy sons, and thy wife, and thy sons wives with thee.
Eight: Means new beginning, new life, a new creation.

Genesis 7:1-24
Noah and his wife, three sons and their wives count as eight (new beginning) people went into the ark, Not only did God tell Noah to build the ark, he told him he would save his family also, Why? Because of Noah's faithfulness and righteousness. He told Noah to take two each kind of animals, male and female. Then God told Noah to take seven good kind of animals to take into the ark (seven: perfection, completion). Can you imagine never seeing rain before, then God tells you to build an ark for he was sending rain upon the earth? God told him it would rain for forty days and forty nights (Forty; trials and testing). Not only were the windows of heaven opened up; the fountains of the deep broke up, it looked like the ocean plate moved or broke and the water came up from the earth as well as from the clouds in the sky. Noah without a shadow of a doubt preached one hundred years (not 120 years like it has been preached, 100 meaning children of the promise) that God was going to bring a rain, people scoffed at him, no doubt laughed and said RAIN! What is that! They went their own way, eating, drinking and marrying. God has an ARK today, it is call ***THE ARK OF SAFETY: JESUS IS THE ARK OF SAFETY:*** Jesus is our refuge our hiding place. God is calling all his people to come into the Ark of Safety. Then Noah opened up the window sent out a raven, then he sent out a dove; which represents the spirit, as Jesus was baptized by John when Jesus came up out of the water the spirit descending on Jesus in a form of a dove.

Psalms 91: 1-4
He that dwells in the secret place of the Most High shall abide under the shadow of the Almighty.
2nd I will say of the Lord, He is my refuge and my fortress my God; in him will I trust.
3rd Surely he shall deliver thee from the snare of the fowler, and from the noisome pestilence.
4th He shall cover thee with his feathers, and under his wings shalt thou trust; his truth shall be thy shield and buckler.

Feathers (Hebrew) protection, strong joint of the body to the wing. To take flight, to soar.
Refuge (Hebrew) shelter, hope, trust
Buckler (Hebrew) wall, large shield, target
Shadow (Hebrew) shade, defense

When we come into the Ark of Safety, which is Jesus Christ, under his wing is the place of safety. We are under the strong joint, which supplies our need, we under his shadow which is a shade of protection and defense. God is calling all his people to come into the Ark of Safety to come unto him who are burdened and heavy laden I will give you rest, for He is our Rest!

Revelation 3:20
Behold (look) I stand at the door (our heart) and knock; if any man hear my voice, and open up the door, I will come *into Him,* and will sup with him, and him with me.

We are to enter into the Ark of safety as Noah entered into the ark. Jesus is the Ark, he wants us to enter so he can enter into us.

Praise of Wisdom:

Proverbs 8:1-30
Doth not **Wisdom** cry? (call, proclaim) And understanding put forth her voice?
2nd She standeth in the top of high places, by the way in the places of the paths.
5th O ye simple, understand **Wisdom**: and ye fools, be ye of an understanding heart
30th I was daily in His delight, rejoicing always before Him.

When we are praising Him in our daily life with the Lord, we are His delight. He longs for us to praise him with a whole heart, and a joyous heart, to enter into His presence. We like to be acknowledged by our children, given praise and to hear how much they love us instead of constantly hearing I want this and I want that, and for them to be begging for every little thing they want. We would have a broken heart if our children rejected everything we try to do for them, this is how the Lord feels about us also.

Psalms 111:1-10
Praise ye the Lord with all my whole heart, in the assembly of the upright and in the congregation.
2nd The works of the Lord are great, sought out of all them that have pleasure therein.
5th He hath given meat unto them that fear him: he will never be mindful of His covenant.

What the Lord is saying here is: give your all to me and I will give my all to you. Well I would say this here is not a fair exchange considering I have nothing but myself to give, and He has given his all to me.

I do not see why we cannot give our all to him; for he has given lot more to us than we could ever give or do for him in our lifetime. What an honor and a privilege that he would give us his Kingdom to rule and reign with him through all eternity. And we cannot even give him our heart, mind soul, and strength.

The Strength and Price of Wisdom:

Proverbs 3:13
Happy is the man that finds **Wisdom**, and the man that gets understanding.
14th For the merchandise of it is better than the merchandise of silver, and gain thereof than fine gold.
15th She is more precious than rubies; all things thou canst desire are not to be compared unto her.

In other word riches cannot compare to **Wisdom**, She is priceless, She is above rubies, her merchandise is worthy and very costly; they are a priceless, they are a price to pay to get **Wisdom**. You can only obtain her through the riches of The Lord Jesus Christ. When we find her we find wealth untold. We can be the wealthiest person on this planet but it will not buy **Wisdom**. The wealth of this world will not buy happiness, love, or family. We can be wealthy and still be unhappy. I have seen poor people just as happy or happier for they have love, joy and happiness in the Lord. I am not saying we cannot be rich, I am saying we must be rich in the Lord.

We must have strength of **Wisdom** to build the house with each other, the strength to build on the Rock, for the Lord Jesus is our Rock.

The Benefits of Wisdom:

Proverbs 4:5-10
Get **Wisdom**, get understanding; forget it not; neither decline from the words of my mouth.
6th Forsake her not, and she shall preserve thee, love her and keep thee.
7th **Wisdom** is the principal thing: therefore get **Wisdom** with all thy getting get understanding.
8th Exalt her, and she shall promote thee: she shall bring thee to honor, when thou dost embrace her.
9th She shall give to thine head an ornament of grace: a crown of glory shall be many.

When we receive **Wisdom**, we receive understanding also. We are not to forget where it came from. Not turn away from or reject what the Lord has given to us. We are not only to receive **Wisdom** and understanding we are to embrace it with everything in us. We are to exalt her, in other words lift her up to bring honor that is due her. We are adding not only years to our lives we are adding benefits; a crown of life! A crown of glory, promotions into his Kingdom, His Grace for it is sufficient.

Keeps Us, Guides Us:

Ecclesiastes 5:1-6
Keep thy foot when thou go to the house of God, and be more ready to hear, than to sacrifice of fools: for they consider not that they do evil.
4th When thou vow a vow unto God, defer not to pay it, for he has no pleasure in fools.

6th Suffer not thy mouth to cause thy flesh to sin: neither say thou before the angel, that it was an error: wherefore should God be angry at thy voice, and destroy the work of thy hands?

Keep thy foot, this is to keep our feet on the **Solid Rock (Jesus Christ)** In other words, stay rooted and grounded in the Word of God. Be ready to receive, to learn to know it is of God or not, know them that labor among you. We are not to open our mouth unless the Holy Ghost speaks through us. We are to be watchful of our mouth before we speak. We are to watch what we speak or vow before the Lord. Are we in a feel good flesh mode, or did God speak. When God speaks it will line up with the Word. If does not line up with the word, you are the same as a fool. When we make vows and we break them it becomes a lie, not only a lie but it comes under thief how is that? When we make a pledge and we break it the people is counting on that money so think before you pledge. The truth is strong and it cuts and it hurts. But it will make you free. Use **Wisdom and understanding;** it will keep you from evil.

Wisdom gives Life:

Ecclesiastes 7:19
Wisdom strengthens the wise more than ten mighty men which are in the city.

Wisdom is not only wise but she gives us strength among men in large crowds. Rely on God's **Wisdom** (not our earthly **Wisdom**) it will give courage to go with our strength in the Lord.

Stability in Wisdom:

Isaiah 33:5-6
The Lord is exalted; for he dwells on high: he has filled Zion with righteousness.
6th And **Wisdom** and knowledge shall be thy **Stability** of thy times, and strength of thy salvation: the **Fear** of the Lord is his treasure.

The Lord's treasure is; his people having **Fear** of him. This fear he is talking about is; having reverence and honor that is due him. The Lord is to be exalted on high from where the blessings flow. This **Wisdom** and Knowledge is our stability our strength of our salvation. We are the Lord's treasure. How much more awesome can this get!

Wisdom Produces Good Fruit:

James 3:17-18
Wisdom that is from above is first pure, then peaceable, gentle, and easy to be intreated, full of mercy and good fruits, without partiality, and hypocrisy.
18th And the fruit of righteousness is sown in peace of them that make peace.
Intreated (Greek) persuasion.

You cannot get away from **Wisdom** it is in every aspect of the way. **Wisdom** is knowledge brings understanding; it is first pure, peaceable, persuades you to enter in the treasures of **Wisdom**. **Wisdom** is without partiality, hypocrisy, she gives good fruit, sown in peace, brings righteousness in the Holy Ghost. **Wisdom** you could write on through to eternity and keep on going, **Wisdom** is endless. Many people have taught, ministered and written on **Wisdom**. We are coming together one by one teaching one another, God is opening up **Wisdom** more and more to his people, for they are seeking. Adam cannot stand the Rhema Word (Spirit), it destroys him. He can take the logos the written word; Adam can stand. The spirit man within us is rising up hearing the words of **Wisdom** and he is understanding what the spirit is saying to his church. Arise Shine; for light is come, arise shine! His light shining in us; and through us. Praise the Lord we are more than conquers in Jesus Christ. We are entering into a more perfect day. We are covered through and by His blood.

Worldly Wisdom Verses Godly Wisdom:

I Corinthians 19-21
For it is written, I will destroy the **Wisdom** of the wise, and will bring to nothing of the understanding of the prudent.
20th Where is the wise? Where is the scribe? Where is the disputer of this world? Hath not God made foolish of the **Wisdom** of this world?
21st For after that in the *Wisdom* of God the world by **Wisdom** knew not God, it pleased God by the foolishness of preaching to save them that believe.
Prudent (Greek) mentally putting together, to comprehend, to be wise.

This is flesh speaking not the spirit. The Sadducee's and Pharisees had great **Wisdom** but they had not the spiritual aspect of spiritual things. Their **Wisdom** destroyed more than it helped. They were under the law they could not see the spiritual things set before them, the law brings death not life, if the law brought life then Grace would not have had to come. Their **Wisdom** and God's **Wisdom** are two different things.

If we preach unto lost souls by man's ways seems foolish. Worldly **Wisdom** verses God's **Wisdom**, worldly **Wisdom** brings death not life, God's **Wisdom** brings life. We are wise when we rely on God's **Wisdom**, it brings peace, it is pure and from above.

Self-Glory:

Jeremiah 9:23-24
Thus saith the Lord, let not the wise man glory in his **Wisdom**, neither let the might man glory in his might, let not the rich man glory in his riches.
24th But let him that glories glory in this, that he understands and knows me, and *I am* the Lord that exercise loving kindness,, and righteousness, in the earth: for in these things I delight, say the Lord.

The only glory that we are to have is the Lord's; we are only mighty through him, the only glory we are to know is the Lord God's glory. We are not to be puffed up or pat ourselves on the back, it is not about us it is about him, being the King of Glory. When we see ourselves and not God we are not humble, we are prideful; and we want to be seen as the Sadducee's and Pharisees were seen. Do not say: I did this, there is only one *I Am!* We all have been guilty of this one time or another, if we see this happening back up and say: Lord help me. We can say God sent me and I did what he sent me to do.

God Given:

For I will give you a mouth and **Wisdom**, which all your adversaries shall not be able to gain say nor resist.

The Lord gave us His **Wisdom** to know when to speak, when to keep silent, we will know when to speak, and what to say in the hour we are to speak. When we speak in the right spirit, the right time they will not be able to resist the **Wisdom** we speak, it will leave them speechless.

One of the gifts as I said earlier is The Gift of **Wisdom**. There is also the gift of Knowledge by the same spirit. We as a body have all there is of God coming together bone of his bone, fitly joined together unto the head, (Jesus Christ) then we will have **<u>ONE NEW MAN! NO MORE TWAIN (TWO)</u>.**

Ephesians 1:17
That the God of our Lord Jesus Christ, the Father of glory, may give unto you the spirit of **Wisdom** and **Revelation** in the **knowledge** of Him.

The gifts of the spirit are given by: God the Father. The Lord is revealing to the body every good thing from above, as we are maturing in Him.

Praying For:

Colossians 1:9
For this cause we also since the day we heard it, do not cease to pray for you, and to desire that ye might be filled with the knowledge of his will in all **Wisdom** and spiritual understanding.

Not only are we to desire **Wisdom** to have his knowledge with understanding, we are to desire our brethren to have them also. When we see lack in our brethren, we should have a desire and the love of God to pray for them with all sincerity. This is called brotherly love, a Godly love.

The Lack of:

James 1:5-6,8
If any of you lack **Wisdom**, let him ask of God, that gives to all men liberally, and unbraided not; and it shall be given.
There is no excuse to be in lack, or be in wanting. All we have to do is ask God and he will give you the desires of your heart. (Luke 12:32-it is his good pleasure to give you the Kingdom).

6th But let him ask in faith not wavering. For he that wavers is like a wave of the sea driven with the wind and tossed.

8th A double minded man is unstable in all his ways!

When we waver not, we are on solid ground, rooted and steady, unmovable. We are a tree that is planted deep in the ground. Our roots run deep and it keeps us steady through the storms of life. This is real faith not tossed about with every wind and doctrine that comes into our path.

When we are not rooted and grounded in the Word we are the same as a double minded. We cannot believe one thing one day and change our mind when someone says they believe this way. This is different when the Lord reveals a Word to us and we get our mind changed. When the Lord enlightens us in the Word we will not back down, we will stand on it regardless what comes against us. If you come across a double minded person in the Word, nine chances out of ten he is unstable in the natural things of his life. We are to stay in the word, to study to read and run reference for there is life in the word. It becomes our life, our stability, our lifestyle. There is no reason for lack in the Kingdom of God.

Notes

Chapter 5

People who Learn This Fear Are Few

The Results of Rejecting:

Proverbs 11:8-23
The righteous is delivered out of trouble, and the wicked comes in his stead.
9th An hypocrite with his mouth destroys his neighbor: but through knowledge shall the just be delivered.
12th He that is void is (empty) of **Wisdom** despises his neighbor: but a man of understanding holds his peace.
13th A talebearer, reveals secrets: but he that is of a faithful spirit conceals the matter.
23rd The desire of the righteous is only good: but the expectation of the wicked is wrath.

James 3:8-10
The ***Tongue*** no man can tame; it is unruly evil, full of deadly poison.
10th Out of the same mouth proceeds blessings and cursing. My brethren these things ought not be.

We cannot tame our tongue! It is not in us to control it. It is Adam's nature to put blame on someone else. It is called passed the buck. When God called Adam and asked where he was, Adam said: I am naked! Who told you that you were naked? This woman you gave me! See he is not taking blame here; he is blaming the woman, as you look a little closer he is putting blame on God. The woman you gave me, in other words I would not have fell if you did not give me this woman. This is our fleshly nature to pass the buck, never to take blame ourselves, that is not going to happen. We have a nature in us to see no wrong in our own eyes, it takes the Holy Ghost to reveal ourselves to us. The tongue here; it reveals secrets, such as we go and tell someone about a secret someone shared, think it is alright for we are going to pray for this person, and we need to know how to pray. The tongue has split churches, families, and friends. The tongue has no bones in it, but it breaks up lives and destroys. You can be in a moment of hurt, or anger, go out in a wind storm rip open a feather pillow,and the wind sweep them up in a whir-wind then you regret it, try to catch them and put them back in the pillow case it is not going to happen. When we get hurt we are to let the Holy Ghost hold our tongue like a bit in a horse's mouth. When we hold our tongues, and we conceal or keep it to ourselves causes peace in our lives. The Holy Ghost is the only way to bridle our tongues, believe me I have went to say something and the Holy Ghost has stopped me a few times over the years. So we see here, we can be a wholesome, peaceful person lead of the Holy Ghost, or we can be a wicked talebearer that speaks lies and spread rumors.

The Holy Ghost and the Holy Spirit is different; I know this is different than what you ever heard before. The Holy Spirit is the (Hebrew) the Old Testament. The Holy Spirit was given to the very elect and they were not baptized with this Holy Spirit, the Holy Spirit was on them as it was needed. It speaks of the Holy Spirit in the Four Gospels for the four Gospels are still under the Law: but in the New Testament it speaks of the birth of Christ but still under the law. Then Jesus told his disciples: St. John 16:7-8. Nevertheless I tell you the truth; it is expedient for you that I go away; for if I go not away, the comforter **WILL NOT COME!** Unto you; but if I depart, I will send him unto you. 8th And when he is come, he will reprove the world of sin, and of righteousness, and of.

So let us go to Acts

Acts 2:1-4
And when the day of Pentecost was **FULLY COME**, they were all with one accord in one place.
2nd And suddenly there came a sound from heaven as of a rushing mighty wind, and it filled all the house where they were sitting.
3rd And there appeared unto them cloven tongues as of fire, and it sat upon each of them.
4th And they were **FILLED** with the **HOLY GHOST**, and began to speak with other tongues, as the spirit gave them utterance.
Accord (Greek) United, in togetherness, as one, with one, agree.
Cloven (Greek) distribute, to divide, parted among.
Filled (Greek) to be full, fulfilled, perfect, complete, accomplish, supply.

When Jesus went away he sent back the comforter as he promised the disciples. The comforter is the Holy Ghost; a Ghost has had to live before, which is Jesus Christ the spirit of the living God. The Holy Spirit is (Hebrew) and it was a select few who had it. The Holy Ghost is for all, and who is filled and baptized in the Holy Ghost. The Holy Ghost leads and guides us in all truth. That is what keeps our tongues bridled. Jesus' own Mother had to be there also, she was not exempt Acts 1:14 She was commanded as well as the others to be there.

Acts 1:4-14
And they assembled together with them, commanded them they should not depart from Jerusalem but wait for the promise of the Father, saith he, ye have heard of me.

8th but ye shall receive POWER after the Holy 'Ghost is come upon you,

When they assembled together ten days before the Holy Ghost came, they were all in one agreement. They were united and all came as one then on the tenth day they were filled and baptized, they were full and the Holy Ghost accomplished and supplied their need.

Six Things That God Hates and Seven is an Abomination Unto him:

Proverbs 6:16-19
1. A proud look
2. A Lying tongue
3. Hands that shed innocent blood
4. A heart that Devises Wicked Imaginations
5. Feet that be swift in running to Mischief
6. A false witness that speaks lies
7. He that sows discord among the brethren

1. **A Proud Look**:

   There is pride when we have a; like look at me syndrome. Look and see what I have done, or look what I have. Pride; pride gives a false pretense, it brings damnation to our soul, it will cause us to lose out in the end. It has happened to us all one time or another, God gets us back in control when we listen.

Proverbs 11:2
When pride comes, then comes shame; but with lowly is **Wisdom.**

James 4:6-But he gives more grace. Wherefore he says. God resists the proud, but gives grace to the humble.

2. **A lying tongue**:

Genesis 3:4
And the serpent said unto the woman, ye shall surely die.

Genesis 4:9
And the Lord said unto Cain, Where is Able thy brother> I know not; Am I my brother's keeper.

Acts 5:1-10
But a certain man Ananias with Sapphira his wife, sold a possession.
2nd and kept back part of the price, his wife being privy to it, and brought a certain part, and laid it at the apostle's feet.

You can read all ten verses here, you will find they not only lied to the apostles, they lied to the Holy Ghost. They sold their land and did not give all they promised and lied. They did not give all they had promised, so they lied, they were deceitful. This brought their own death, they both had died instantly one by one. Cain lied, said he knew not where his brother was, knowing he killed him. Then the serpent lied told Eve she would not die if she partook of the fruit. There are several different lies here, told differently, but any way you look at it, it is still lying.

3. **Hands That Shed Innocent Blood**:

II Samuel 1:14-16
And David said unto him, thy blood be upon thy head: for thy mouth testified against thee, saying, I have slain the Lord's anointed.

I Kings 18:4
For it was so, when Jezebel cut off the prophets of the Lord, that Obadiah took an hundred prophets, and hid them by fifty (Jubilee, Pentecost) in a cave, and fed them with bread (Word) and (spirit) water.
II Kings 9:10-27 (Read all of these verses)

Jezebel was an evil woman and tried to kill, and seduce the prophets of God through her false gods of Baal. Jezebel promotes all evil things, she not only seduces, she manipulates, works in power and control issues. She is in the churches today teaching lies, seducing the prophets, causing them to fall. She has rocked the church to sleep with heresy doctrine.
Jezebel (Greek) A false teacher.

Revelation 2:20-23
Notwithstanding I have a few things against thee, because thou suffers that woman Jezebel, which called herself a prophetess, to teach, and seduce my servants to commit fornication, and eat things sacrificed unto idols.

That Jezebel spirit is still in the secular church world. The Jezebel-harlot is a spirit of self, it is idolatry of self-love.

Philippians 2:21
For all seek their own, not things which are ***Jesus Christ's.***

The harlot spirit is present when we try to build something on feeling or flesh. The Jezebel spirit is murderous and not only leads people astray but she destroys the sonship. Not only false doctrines taught, we are letting in the new age movement. There is a lust spirit that is causing divorcement in the church world. The ministers are lusting after things that are leading them astray. We are to be watchful not to put ourselves in a place that we let the enemy come in and be lead astray.

Let us go back to Genesis 4:9 Where Cain killed his brother. Cain was jealous of his brother, Abel's sacrifice; for God took his Brother Abel's offering and did not take his. Instead of Cain going back and giving a blood sacrifice, he become jealous and went into a rage of jealousy slew his brother. This still happens today. People kill for less, they kill for revenge, money jealousy, or in the fear of being exposed. We must be careful we do not let the devil control us, it causes us to do things we normally do not or would not do. When we ask for forgiveness the Lord forgives us, but we must still pay the price of what we have done. Take for instance if we have broken the law and we get caught we still have to pay the penalty of the crime we committed. Is the price worth the penalty?

Matthew 15:18-20
For out of the heart proceed evil thoughts, murderers, adulteries, fornications, thefts, false witness, blasphemies

20th these are the things which defile a man: but to eat with unwashed hands defiles not a man.

Mark 7:21-23
For from within, out of the heart of men, proceed evil thoughts, adulteries, fornications, murders.
22nd theft, covetousness, wickedness, deceit, lasciviousness an evil eye, blasphemy, pride, foolishness;
23rd All these things come from within and defile a man.

Matthew 15:11
Not that which goes in the mouth defiles a man; but that which comes out of the mouth, defiles a man.

The bible says; out of the heart the mouth speaks, the heart of a man speaks his thoughts, desires, and his wants.
Lasciviousness (Greek) sensuality, lewdness, filthy, wantonness.
Blasphemy (Greek) slander, malicious talk, railings, hurtful speech, insult, curse, evil spoken of.

We are to come to the Lord we are to give him our heart, our mind, our soul, to him for our deliverance and our salvation. The defilements; can be destroyed only by the blood that Jesus shed on Calvary. We are to make him Lord of our mind, soul and our heart. We cannot save ourselves it takes Jesus' blood to cover our sins; Past, present, and future.

4. **A heart that Deviseth Wicked Imaginations:**

    Heart (Hebrew) the inner person self, seat of thought and emotion

Deviseth (Hebrew) to plot against, keep silent, conceal, to be cunning, purpose.
Wicked (Hebrew) evil, iniquity, an evildoer, trouble, mischief, false, idols.
Imaginations (Hebrew) A thought plan, plot design, thoughts

The heart is the center of our emotions, where our thought pattern resides. This will bring out the inner person which is our-self. Our thoughts can and will control us if we allow it to do so. We can allow our thoughts to plot against someone we are jealous of, or who have hurt us in times past. We can have a purpose in our heart to plot or conceal what we have in mind to do such as: to get even with someone, to conceal or be cunning then open fire on them to destroy them for various reasons. The wicked thoughts we have in our heart are evil and yes we can destroy people who have hurt us but we destroy ourselves in the process. This evilness does not just happen, it has to first become a thought in our mind and in our heart. We dwell on the matter, then we start to plot and evil steps in and then it is no longer an imagination it has become reality. So when we find ourselves devising or plotting then we need to stop it and replace our thoughts by praying asking God to replace our wicked imagination with the Word.

5. **Feet That Be Swift in Running To Mischief:**

Isaiah 59:7
Their feet to run to evil, and they make haste to shed innocent blood: their thoughts of iniquity; wasting and destruction are in their paths.

Proverbs 1:15
My son walk not thou in the way with them; refrain thy foot from their path.

You come across people in your life that will gossip, lie, and try to destroy you. You are not to mingle with these people, they will destroy your influence. All you can do is let your light shine and do not talk about them only talk to the Lord about their soul. When you walk with a person that lies, steal or gossip, it will weaken your faith. You cannot run with a gossiper eventually you will become one of them. We are not to let our ears be garbage cans. This is very dangerous, a gossiper is same as a murderer, for they kill peoples influence. A gossiper is very dangerous person, they are cunning, they will call you and tell you to pray for someone and tell everything they know about the person and then some so you can pray for them, this is not godly, it is a form of deceit. This is the reason we are to have the Holy Ghost we are to know who labors among us.

6. **A False Witness That Speaks Lies**:

Exodus 20:16
Thou shalt not bear false witness against thy neighbor.

This is the ninth commandment. We must speak with all fairness and a just matter. This is a commandment that speaks of lies, we speak one lie we will speak another lie to cover up the first lie, it is a snowball effect down-hill, it just keeps getting bigger as it rolls down- hill.

Exodus 23:1-2

Thou shalt not raise a false report: put not thine hand with the wicked to be unrighteous witness.

2nd Thou shalt not follow multitudes to do evil; neither shalt thou speak in a cause to decline after many to wrest judgment.

Wrest (Hebrew) overthrow, turn away, to spread out.

Numbers 13:31-33

And they brought up an evil report of the land which thy had searched unto the children of Israel, saying, the land, through which we have gone to search it, is a land that eats up the inhabitants thereof; and all the people that we saw in it are men of great stature.

33rd And there we saw giants, the sons of A'nak, which come of the giants: and **we were in our own sight as grasshoppers**. (flesh) and so *we were in their sight.*

Numbers 14:1-2-37

And all the congregation lifted up their voice and cried; and the people wept that night

2nd And all the children of Israel murmured against Moses and against Aaron: and the whole congregation said unto them, would God that we had died in the land of Egypt! Or would God we had died in this wilderness!

37th Even those men that did bring up the evil report upon the land ***DIED!*** By the plague before The Lord.

Moses sent out the spies to spy out the land, Caleb and Joshua saw the same thing but they went in the spirit and saw the spiritual side, where the other spies looked in the natural realm they brought an evil report (death) all who heard cried all night then they died. When Joshua and Caleb came back they gave a good report all who heard lived. This is why we must watch what our ears hear and our eyes see. Life and death is in the power of the tongue. We must hear what the spirit is saying to our church. We hear evil as well as speak it brings death. We are to watch that we do not hear of an evil report.

7. **He That sows Discord Among His Brethren**:

Proverbs 6:14
Frowardness is in his heart, he devise mischief continually; he sows discord.
Discord (Hebrew) strife, brawling and contention

We are causing trouble, among our brothers and sisters, quarreling with one another, bringing anger and frustration between ourselves. This brings division and a lot of hurt, it destroys families, churches and friendships. Discord has destroyed cities, countries, and people's lives. This has brought wars and murders, I could go on forever what discord has brought in our lives. We are to keep in continual prayer and watch what we say before we speak. Speak with seasoned words, in other words use **Wisdom** before you speak, think and let the Holy Ghost speak through you. The secular church world is trying to be under Grace; teach the law; put you in bondage, No one person has it all, or knows it all, we all err; but as we grow and mature in God we learn from our own lessons of life we have had to walk. We learn lessons in life by the things we have suffered; such as trials, testing, and mountains we have climbed, deserts we have walked, this is where we gain **Wisdom** through all these things and places we have walked in our Christian walk. We help one another through our sufferings. When **Wisdom** prevails with knowledge and understanding we can assemble together and feed one another.

Let me tell you of my experience when I was in my early twenties, when I rededicated my life back to the Lord. I went back to the only way I knew was true holiness. I got to the place I could no longer feel the Holy Ghost in my life. I got down on my knees and asked the Lord Why I could not feel the Holy Ghost anymore. Then the Lord spoke into my spirit and told me to take the mask off, I looked up the word mask, I cried "Lord you called me a hypocrite." He proceeded to tell me I let man mold me, holiness is on the inside it has nothing to do with how long your hair or your dress is, or wearing pants or makeup, and the men with their long sleeves or clean shaven, it has got a lot to do with the condition of your heart. Then I began to pray for the Lord to clear my mind of man's traditions and teach me, I did not understand at the time what I prayed, but in time I realized there was a price to pay for this Word. There has been many trials, valleys, and mountains I have climbed and many rejections along the way, this made me cry out to the Lord all the more and to get alone with God. In the alone times with God he revealed His Word to me, woke me up in the still of the night to give me a Word. **Wisdom** will mature you, give you the knowledge the understanding, it is a wellspring springing up within your very soul.
The Letter (law) kills, but the Spirit makes alive. There is life in the Word.

Apostle Paul said: Our spirit is willing but our flesh is weak. Our nature is weak and lazy. Our old Adam nature wants to play games, watch TV go shopping, read the newspaper or a book, when it comes time to lay aside our pleasures of life we are tired, or we do not have time. I am not condemning anyone for pleasures of life, there is nothing wrong with it, but we do not make time for God in our lives. We should get up a few minutes early to have morning devotion, to read a scripture and run a few references and to pray before our day begins. We will find our spirit is refreshed, and feel better in our spirit. When we look back a year later we can see progress, we can write down the scripture we read every day; go back and we may have a greater insight on what we have read or studied. We can get ourselves in a routine every morning like a runner does. When he gets up in the morning he gets up very early way before breakfast and prepare to run, he runs a few miles before daybreak. This becomes him, he will not let nothing come in the way of his running this is his life. When we get that way with our Lord in the mornings it becomes us, it is our way of life. There are some people who is not a morning person or their jobs are different, they work second or third shift, they will walk or run at night, they can do their devotions and prayer before or after work, it don't matter as long as we put God first and foremost in our walk with the Lord. This comes easier as it becomes a daily routine, we will began to learn, to get stronger in our devotion to the Lord. When you plan a trip you just do not get in a car or plane and go, they are preparations and reservations to make. We make phone calls to motel, we book a flight we get our clothes ready, if we drive we must map out the directions we do not get in a car and go. This is the way it is on our journey to heaven, we must make preparations. We got our bibles, we got our prayer-line, and we got reservations made, we know one day after while we will depart for that journey and we must be ready. Apostle Paul said this is a pressing way, we are running a race it is not how fast we run, it is how we endure with patience.

The Fool

Proverbs 13:15-16
Good understanding giveth favour: but the way of transgressors is hard.
16th Every prudent man deals with knowledge: but a fool lays open his folly
Transgressor (Hebrew) unfaithful, to betray, deceitful,
Prudent (Hebrew) wise, understanding and clever.
Folly (Hebrew) foolishness

As we see here: the way of an unfaithful, deceitful person is a hard road to walk. A very wise person take the knowledge he has puts understanding with it for he is clever, and he lives what he knows through his studies in the bible. But when a fool opens his mouth he reveals who he is, and his way is foolish.

Proverbs 14:8-9
The **Wisdom** of the prudent (wise) is to understand his way: but folly of fools is deceit.
9th Fools make a mock at sin; but among the righteous there is I.

Proverbs 17:28
Even a fool, when he holds his peace, is counted wise: and he that shuts his lips is esteemed a man of understanding.

Proverbs 18:2-7
A fool hath no delight in understanding, but that his heart may discover itself.
7th A fools mouth is his destruction, and his lips are the snare of his soul.

Fool (Hebrew) stupid, silly, foolish, Webster's dictionary, a silly person; a windbag, a simpleton.

We must watch what we say, before we speak. We must season our words with love. When we speak without knowledge and **Wisdom** we will destroy anything and everything in our path. A fool just opens his mouth and speaks whatever will come out of his mouth. Have you ever heard the old saying; a person that talks too much says nothing? I met a few people like that, they just rattle off and I have no clue what the person is talking about. A fool knows no restraint, he just rattles on. Believe it, or not! This has happened in the church world; the leaders do not set them aside to teach them to get them ready for the ministry, to know the whole salvation plan. They do not teach them to know the basics of the Bible, to know how to study the Bible or know how to run a reference. The person gets in too deep, then they fall by the way for they become as a fool. We need to pray before we go to church, get our mind on the Lord and lay aside our troubles of the day to know in the spirit the right song to sing, what message is needed for the hour. We must know the leading of the spirit, to know when to speak when to sing when to keep silent, we learn this through studying through prayer, to be still and listen to what the spirit is saying. I have seen where ministers have built up churches fast, working hard they have the drawing power but in a moment they tear down what it took them a year to build, Why? They did not use **Wisdom**, they did not have the knowledge or the understanding to build on. I am not trying to condemn anyone, or thank no one knows nothing, I am telling you what I have seen over the years, to open people's eyes to the seriousness of the matter. We all have missed it, or hurt someone, opened our mouth and hurt someone, we all have acted as fools, and I believe most of us have learned great lessons on our blunders or foolishness. I have set on my gift and callings for years for I have seen flesh work, people thinking they are in the spirit. I am not saying I have not erred I have, but God has quickened me to let me know I messed up. I watch carefully now, not quick to move or speak. I still can err as well as they next person, that is why we must keep the reverent fear of the Lord continually.

Proverbs 12:15
The way of a fool is right in our own eyes: but he that hearkened unto counsel is wise.

You cannot prove a fool wrong, for he is righteous in his own eyes. I do not care how much proof you have to prove a fool wrong he will not hear you.

Proverbs 29:11
A fool Utters All his Mind, but a wise man keeps it in till after-words.

Matthew 7:3
And why behold thou the mote (speck) that is in thy brother's eye, but considers not the beam (plank) that is in thy own eye.

In other words a speck is very hard to see, while a plank or beam is about as big as your whole body. It shows here that it only takes the Holy Ghost to reveal yourself to you. A lot of times we are the last to see our wrong doings, that is scary, then sometimes we are too hard on ourselves. When this happens this cuts us to the core. Believe me I got some pretty hard and harsh words from the Lord, and they have not been soft.

The Scoffer

Proverbs 9:7-8
He that reproves a scorner gets to himself shame: and he that rebukes a wicked man gets himself a blot.
8th Reprove not a scorner, lest he hate thee: rebuke a wise man and he will love thee.

Reprove (Hebrew) to reason together, same as rebuke.
Scorner (Hebrew) A mocker, to jeer at, make a mock
Rebuke (Hebrew) discipline, chastened, correct
Scoffer (Greek) A false teacher, mock, to jeer at

He that reasons together; to discipline or to correct a scorner (mocker) brings to himself shame. The person that disciplines or corrects a wise man, a man with great **Wisdom** he will love thee, why? It brings life to his soul.

Proverbs 1:22
How long, ye simple ones, will ye love simplicity? And the scorners delight in your scorning, and fools hate knowledge.

Did you notice that the fool, scoffer and the scorner go hand in hand with each other?

11 Peter 3:3
Knowing this first, that there shall come in the last days scoffers, walking after their own lusts.

Galatians 6:7
Be not deceived: God is not mocked: for whatever a man sows; that shall he also reap.

The Last Days started on the Day of Pentecost. If you have done any kind of studying you will have already have seen this. Scoffers are false teachers, telling their deceits. They lust after their own words. They have not the spirit of the true living God. They have false teaching and lead people astray. They say they have studied with the most famous, and the best they put their false doctrines in their spirit not getting in the Bible for themselves, preaching false doctrine and leading people astray. This is very dangerous, for we will stand for every error we have taught. We must be careful or we are letting ourselves be as scoffers.

Proverbs 19:29
Judgments are prepared for scorners, and stripes for the back of fools.

(Hebrew) Divine law, to be judged, ordinance, verdict, measure, pronounce sentence for or against, to condemn, execute.

The final and most heart rendering here is a dose of their own medicine. They seek after their own way. I have seen many people stay in their own deceit for the fear of rejection, they would rather flow in their own spirit. I would rather take the rejection of the people than to reject God's way. It is not popular to go against the grain of salt par-say. You do not need to go out of the church world to see scoffers and scorners they are right in the church, they say it is my way or no way. You cannot get them to see the need for change. It is given only by the illumination of the Holy Ghost. We do not condemn them we are to pray for them. We pray for the Lord to open their eyes.

For those who lay claim to the new birth experience of being born again, bought and purchased by and through the blood of the Lamb, to be Christ's followers to be Christ (anointed) in the earth, we sowing in the spirit. When we walk in the spirit, we will fulfilled Christ in the earth and we will not sow to the flesh. We will not desire the works of the flesh.

The Sluggard

In Proverbs: The sluggard is a figure of tragic comedy, with his laziness described as: no different than an animal. He is more than anchored to his bed, he is hinged to it.

Proverbs 26:14-16
The sluggard is wiser than his own deceit than seven men than can render a reason.

Proverbs 6:4-11
Give not sleep to thine eyes, nor slumber to thine eyelids.
6th Go to the ant, thou sluggard: consider her way, and be wise.
7th Which having no guide, overseer, or ruler.
9th How long will thou sleep O sluggard? When wilt thou arise out of thy sleep.
Overseer (Hebrew) scribe, ruler, magistrate, officer,

Proverbs 30:25-2
The ants are a people not strong, yet they prepare their meat in the summer.

26th The conies are but a feeble folk, yet they make their houses in the rocks.
27th The locusts have no king, yet they go forth all of them by bands.
28th The spider taketh hold with her hands, and is in kings' palaces.

It is not how strong an individual is, it is being consistent, being prepared, to persevere with all diligence. We are strong in numbers, we get in unity like an army we become stronger. When an army marches they march in unity step by step. The conies; they build their houses on rocks, we must build our house on the Rock of Jesus Christ. The locust we see here are known as coming in groves or in bands, they cannot do in damage to the crops if they are one or two but when they come in bands they are swarms of them they can clear a crop in no time. A spider spins her web in matter of minutes, their web looks feeble but it has a sticky substance the web attracts his enemy, and when they get on the edge of the web the more they try to get out the more trapped they become. So we as an army of God we become stronger in bands, we come in unity of the faith, we come together as one to lift up the blood stein banner of Christ. Our weapons of our warfare are not carnal but mighty to pulling down of strongholds; the weapons **ARE: THE BLOOD, THE WORD, THE NAME**, we must pray, study, it is our life it is our strength in the battle and we will prevail in the Lord.
Sleep (Hebrew) rest, lay self- down, seed, to be slack, to die.

Sleep is a kind of death, just like old Adam, God put him in a deep sleep there was a death that took place. When we are dead to the spirit, we are dead in Adam, we cannot see, or hear what the spirit is saying to our church (heart). We get lazy in our walk with the Lord, it happens to all us. When we get slack, then we start producing death.

1. The Sluggard does not commit himself but he will not refuse, but he will surrender to the smallest task. This is a person who puts off what he or she is to do, in others word they are a procrastinator.
2. He/she will not finish things they have already started. FOR THEY HAVE MANY UNFINSHED TASK.
3. Follows the least difficult task, slothfulness, is it laziness or slothfulness? This is more likely in the spiritual realm then the physical world.
4. The sluggard will not face things in his life, he is like a coward.

The sluggard has all kinds of excuses in his pocket as the old saying goes. He lies so much and so long he begins to believe his own lies, he cannot tell the difference in the truth or the lie. He let the enemy come in take over his mind, his mind is warped and his mind is stunted in the growth of his spirituality.

5. Consequently, the sluggard is restless, he has unfulfilled and unsatisfying desires. He/she runs to and fro to every wind of doctrine, he/she is unstable, unlearned, confused. He/she let their ears hear everything they have no filter, this is dangerous for what we hear gets in our souls this can bring death, remember life and death are in the power of the tongue. What we speak, what we hear must be seasoned with Grace, knowledge must be spoken in **Wisdom**, the understanding or knowing the Word, the rightly divided word. This is what brings life to the Word, to our lives.

The Sluggard's Lesson

Remember the ant? She puts the sluggard to shame. If we would take the example of the ant we would be mighty army.

He is telling us to go to the ant consider her ways, to learn a lesson by watching her work. Have you ever noticed the ant she will carry her food big as she is. The ant will drag it if it is too big to carry in her mouth.

A sluggard will not carry anything too heavy, they will complain, their excuse will be I cannot do it. I have always said; "Can't never did do anything!"

The sluggard is the one you have to plead with, to coach; to stick a fire in under him as the old saying goes. A sluggard will do something if it has something for him in it. I have seen where the sluggard has no vision or goals, they are satisfied with very little, they think of no one but themselves. They will work only if it pleases themselves. One day they see their poverty has arrived his laziness has caught up with them.

Proverbs 6:11
So shall thy poverty come as one that travails, and thy want as an armed man.

There is no arguing with it. Through shirking his/her duties of hard work, he has qualified himself for drudgery. Procrastination has brought him defeat, in every area of his life. The lesson the sluggard learns is nearly too late, he is not only in want he is in great need, no one feel sympathy for him for they have watched him too long, and they will say he brought on himself.

The Sluggard Sees:

The sluggard sees as he feels the pain of need. He is learning through his suffering. He no longer has to be prodded or convinced to work, he feels it through his/her slothfulness and shirking of their duties. When it comes **_EARLY_** spring the farmers are out in their fields preparing for planting. A farmer does not go out and start planting, they must prepare the ground. Then they plant their crops in the right timing, you can plant too early or too late, it is all in the timing. A sluggard fools around till the right time of planting is too late, and they either do not plant or they plant too late and their crops are too immature and die.

Proverbs 24:32
Then I beheld and considered it well: I looked upon it and received instruction.

Psalms 85:4-12
Blessed are they that dwell in thy house; they will be still praising thee, Selah.
5th Blessed is the man whose strength is in thee; in whose heart are the ways of them.
7th They go from strength to strength, *everyone of them in Zion* appears before God.
11th For the Lord God is a *Son* and *Shield:* he will *give Grace and Glory;* no good thing will he withhold from them that walk uprightly.

We see here in scriptures that the fool, the scoffer, and the sluggard go hand in hand. They are like the false balance. We have Wisdom, Knowledge, and Understanding, they go hand in hand this is the true balance.

I John 3:1-3
Behold what manner of love the Father hath bestowed upon us, that we should be called the **_SON'S OF GOD!_** Therefore the world knows us not, because it knew him not.

2nd Beloved now are we the **Sons of God,** and it doth not yet appear what we shall be; but we know that, when he shall appear we shall be **LIKE HIM;**

3rd And every man that hath this hope in him purifies himself, even as he is pure.

Bestowed (Greek) granted, delivered, given.

Romans 8:14
For as many are led by the spirit of God, they are the son of God.

Galatians 4:7
Wherefore thou art no more a servant, but **_A SON;_** and if a SON, then an **_HEIR of GOD though CHRIST!_**

Here is where we miss it, or stunt our growth in the Lord. We have a mentality of a servant. A servant or a slave only has a promise. A child only has the mentality of a child, not an adult. They have no direction, the only direction a child has is their parents. When the child is home they have an inheritance the money is put in an account, they only have a promise of this money. A child would spend their inheritance foolishly they would spend it according to their mentality. A servant or slave can only do as their master lets them they have no need for money for they are under their rule of thumb per say. When we mature and grow in the Lord we are no longer a slave or servant. We become mature (perfect) we have come to the full stature in the Lord. We become a full statured SON! The *body* is rising out of the earth, Jesus (heaven) laying his head upon the shoulders (strength) heaven and earth coming together. The Lord woke me up out of a sound sleep with a big booming voice! "What I am doing in the heaven's I am doing in the Earth" We are the EARTH! Jesus is the HEAVENLIES. The earth is the Lord's and the fullness of it.

Philippians 2:15
That ye may be blameless and harmless, the sons of God, without rebuke, in the midst of a crooked and perverse nation, among whom ye shine as lights in the world.

We are a city set on the hill, whose light shines out in darkness. **Wisdom** cries out in high places she stands at the top of the hill, **Wisdom** speaks in excellence. We are the light of the world for Jesus' light is in us, we are the city. We are the salt of the earth, we have a flavor, the flavor of God. He said taste of me. We are the **Wisdom** it speaks of in Proverbs.

Luke 1:35
And the angel answered and said unto her, the Holy Ghost shall come upon thee, and over shadow thee; therefore also that the holy thing which shall be born of thee shall be called the **SON OF GOD!**
Overshadow (Greek) mount, ascend, embark, arrive into, direction.

Mary conceived of the Holy Ghost; natural and spiritual. She carried the word in her womb, and the Word became flesh, The Messiah, Immanuel, Meaning **GOD WITH US!** I was studying on the cross, and the Lord spoke into my spirit I trembled, "Everything in me is in you" I marveled at his words, I stood quiet, He proceeded to tell me; As Mary was overshadowed by the Holy Ghost and conceived, We are to be conceived of the seed, the masculine spirit of God. We must birth the male child, this birth cannot be breach, it must come head first. The church is birthing a child but it is coming breach, feet first. The head (Christ) must come first or there is death. We must be impregnated with the seed of the Holy Ghost; the Word. We are birthing Sons into His Kingdom.

God came through Mary; for Mary to conceive of the Holy Ghost, to bring forth Immanuel; God with us, to get back to Adam to redeem back what Adam has lost.

Roman 5:10-19
Wherefore, as **<u>by one man sin entered into the world,</u>** and death by sin; and so men, **death passed upon all men,** for that **all have sinned.**
19th **for by one man disobedience** many were made sinners, so by the **obedience of one** shall many be made righteous.

The Prodigal Son Found Favor:

Here we see the slothful, the fool and the sluggard all in one
We can see where he came to the end of self. When he seen he had spent all he had foolishly, did not work, save or invest, he did not have anything to show for his money spent. When he was not only broke, he was in a pig pen slopping with the hogs, (sound familiar?) we all been there. We see a great love being revealed to us and we miss it. The Father seen him afar off, He cried (yelled) he had a love, a compassion for his son, he just came out of a pig pen, dirty, smelly with torn clothes, not fit to look at nether the less hug him and kiss him, to take him in your arms and smell his stench. All he saw was his son was hungry and thirsty, the Father ran to him fell on his neck and he kissed his filthy stinky neck. The son is confessing to his Father with all humility "I have sinned Daddy against you and all of heaven,

I am no more worthy to be called thy son! You know what the Father said? Bring Forth the best (royal) robe, and here is the ring he put it on his finger, and new shoes on his feet (new walk) bring the fatted calf (table spread) **Wisdom** killed her beast, **Wisdom** cried, She prepared the banquet table. She sent forth her maidens in the street (minister). For my son was dead (in sin) and he is alive once more, he was lost, but now he is found. Now we see the elder son is the first son is Jealous. Who is the first born son? The first Adam, he lost his inheritance. Pride puffed him up, he wanted all the Kingdom, wanted to be like God. He took of the tree of good and evil, he will be like God, knowing it all. The elder came to the house he heard them instruments playing people singing and praising God, they were dancing they were rejoicing over one lost sheep. He left the ninety and nine; (mature Christians) to get that one lost little lamb. The elder brother was angry, he could not come in, The Father came out told him about himself.

The blood of Jesus Christ covers all sins. Past, present, Future. He did not come to give half or a small percentage of life, He came to die for ALL mankind. You love your children, you will do everything for your children even if it means your life. That is the love the Lord gave to us, the same love he has for us. It means you have a prefect love for them regardless of their situations in life. He loves the wayward son as well as the good favored son.

John 15:13
Greater love hath no man than this that a man would lay down his life for his friends.

This is true love. The Love of God is a love that knows no ill, Love is patient, love is kind, love is gentle, and is peaceable. This LOVE is the kind of love you will lay your life down and die so the Lord can raise you up in the likeness of him.

John 3:17
For God sent not his son into the world to condemn the world; but that the world through him might be saved.

When Jesus met the woman at the well, he did not condemn her, He could not have condemned her for she was already condemned. The Lord showed her love, a more excellent way. When we condemn we are not showing the Love of the Father, we are giving death. We are not fruit inspectors, we see our brother and sister in need we are to restore them back, we are to pray and see their need is Jesus. We are not too hate, we are to show compassion, to show the love of God. We are to look through the EYE of God, which is single full of light. We see through flesh our two eyes (darkness) we see double, and we are double minded and unstable. We are not to shut up our bowels of compassion for if we do we have lost our first love, which is Jesus Christ.

Psalms 85:4-13
Mercy and Truth are met together; righteousness and peace have kissed each other.
11th Truth shall spring out of the earth (us) and righteousness shall look from heaven (JESUS the HEAD) of the body.
Kiss (Hebrew) a mode of attachment, to catch fire, through the ideal of fastening up. Webster; to touch or caress with lips an act of affection, greeting

When Mercy and Truth have met they have attached themselves in an act of touching with affection or greeting. Then Truth shall spring forth out of love and they go hand in hand. The Lord is truth and the Truth is in us, and the Lord has kissed us with his fire of the Holy Ghost!

John 4:24
God is a spirit and we must worship Him in Spirit and in Truth.

There are Three Things Here:

1. **Worship:** If you do not know the truth you cannot worship, the truth is Jesus Christ.
   St. John 4:22 the true worshipers shall worship the Father in spirit and in truth.
2. **Spirit:** Jesus teaches here: We first come into his gates with thanksgiving, and into his courts with praise; then we must go into the Holy place into the glory realm where the shekinah glory shines and we no longer us it is the God Almighty. This is where it is only the spirit
3. **Truth:** Psalms 31:5
   Into thy hand I commit my spirit: thou hast redeemed me, O Lord God of truth.

   Ephesians 4:15
   But speaking the truth in love, may grow up into him in all things, which is the head, even Christ.

Righteousness:

Proverbs 21:21
He that follow after righteousness, and mercy finds life, and honor.

Matthew 5:6

Blessed are they which hunger and thirst after righteousness: for they shall be filled.

Righteousness (Greek) Trust worthy, assured, establish, faithful, right.

Notes

Chapter 6

To Stand On The Wisdom Of God

Exodus 14:13
And Moses said unto the people, fear ye not, **stand** still, and see the salvation of the Lord, which he will show to you today: for the Egyptians whom ye have seen today, ye shall see them again no more forever.
Stand: Commit one self, present oneself, to stand ones ground, wait establish, placed. (Greek) to be steadfast, be firm.

Moses was informing his people not to fear what the circumstances may look like, look unto God whom is our source. We are not to look at circumstances that stand in our way, for the problem we face can look like there is no way we can be victorious. We are to look up, set our faces like flint, to stand on the Rock (Jesus) the Chief Corner Stone. We are to have **Wisdom** to seek for knowledge; which gives us understanding, that gives us peace. The children of Israel was afraid, as the old saying they are between a rock and a hard place. They looked back they saw the Egyptians coming with their mighty army; with the Red Sea before them. They are not to look back they were to look forward, Luke 9:2; And Jesus said unto him, no man, having put his hand to the plow, and looking back, is fit for the Kingdom of God. As we see here if we look back we see fear, torment, and confusion, we cannot have faith to look forward.

We are lacking faith, we give place to the devil, and we take God out of the equation. The Children of Israel looked to Moses as their leader, Guide, Shepherd over them to take them through. God told Moses to stretch forth his rod over the Red Sea, Just a small rod over such a big vast ocean. Moses had such great faith and great **Wisdom** to know he heard from God. Moses stretched the rod out in faith and God made a wall of water for them to cross over. They were under the protection of the Lord God Almighty, not of what they did, but their shepherd, their leader listening to God to know the voice of God. They followed after Moses with the enemy pursuing behind their back. They saw God letting down the wall of water behind them destroying the enemy at their very heels as he is saving them. This is a form of baptism as the children of Israel passed through the waters into a new place. They were freed from bondage. When we stand still it is not doing nothing, it is letting go and let God lead us. The Israelites witnessed the great miracle the work of the Lord, very powerful.

Exodus 3:5
And he said draw not nigh hither; put thy shoes from thy feet, for the place thereon thou stands is holy ground.
Hither (Hebrew) To here, here.
Nigh (Hebrew) Approach, present, draw, ***stand.***
Draw (Hebrew) Same as nigh

God told Moses to take off his shoes, take off his old way of walking, to approach and present himself before God, for he is in a new place in him. The place where God is taking him is Holy. The Holy Place where Moses is to walk has no room for the past or the old. He said come up hither! He climbed up a steep treacherous mountain to get to that place in God, when he reached the top he was no longer the same man. The place where he is standing is Holy, Moses stood on **Wisdom**, (which is a principle thing). To know what to do by listening to the voice of God; to the knowledge of understanding to go forth in the power of the Lord.

Matthew 7:24
Therefore whosoever hears these sayings of mine and do them, I will liken unto him a wise man, which built his house upon a **_ROCK!_** (Jesus).

We see here in this passage of scripture; we MUST BUILD upon the ROCK (JESUS) of our salvation, which is Jesus Christ the Chief Corner Stone. When we hear, and study the Word of God we are building up our most Holy faith. A wise man will increase in learning, he will hear the Word of the Lord; he will build upon the foundation of the church, for we are the church.

Job 38:36
Who hath put **Wisdom** in the inward parts? Or who hath given understanding to the heart.

Psalms 1:1-3
Blessed is the man that walks not in the counsel of the ungodly, not stands in the way of sinners, not sit in the seat of the scornful.
2nd But his delight is in the law of the Lord; and in his law doth he meditate day and night.
3rd And he shall be like a tree planted by the rivers of water, that brings forth his fruit in his season; his leaf also shall not wither; and whatsoever he does shall prosper.

Whatever we do we must never walk in the counsel of the ungodly, to condemn to bring on evil. We are not to be as the Sadducee and the Pharisees they have **Wisdom** of the world, of self. It is devilish. They bring death, they will put you to death thinking they are doing a just deed. We are to delight or rejoice in the Lord, to be strong as a tree is planted in the river of the water life. To grow up let our leaves bud forth as the tree produces twelve manner of fruit and our leaves fall on one another As Revelation 22:2; says. To heal one another. How? By washing one another with the words of our lips of the Word of God.

Sensual Wisdom:

James 3:14-15
But if you have bitter envying and strife in your hearts, glory not, and lie not against the truth.
15th This **Wisdom** descends not from above, but it is earthly, sensual and devilish.

This is called an evil heart. Full of selfishness, and contention, this **wisdom** is not from God in anyway. This is full of demonic activity, full of lies, this **wisdom** will try to deceive you lie against all truth, gives a little truth to draw you into deceit be careful. There has been times when you are going through a dry season the devil will tell you that you are backslid. We have been told in the church world "If you don't feel it you ain't got it!" This is a faith walk, we are to walk by faith not by sight, yes it is good to feel his spirit, but we do not always feel the spirit. But we have a knowing in our hearts that we are alright. Through our trying of our faith and our trials of fire we are not going to feel anything, but we must praise him, in these trying times. The church world we must be careful who we let in behind the pulpit. They are people who come in to destroy to cause confusion, to bring contention. There is a doctrine if it feels good do it does not matter; our flesh already stinks in the nostrils of God anyway. This is not the truth and it is not the **Wisdom** from above, it is devilish. The devil knows the word, but he distorts it, gives part truths. The devil recognizes God's handiwork, the devils know Jesus when they see him and his work. The devil knows if we are God's people or not. The demonic knowledge and **wisdom** is as follows:

These things are an abomination before the Lord:

Deuteronomy 18:9-12

1. The Horoscope: A chart of the zodiacal signs and positions of the planets time of a person's birth. There is the true Zodiacal signs but there not for us to bother it.
2. Tarot cards: the first tarot cards where the deck of cards. Each symbol has a meaning.
3. Fortune Telling: the eight ball or cards.
4. Palm Reading: Each line in your hand is read, short line, long lines, horizontal or vertical lines.
5. The Crystal Ball: You look into the clear ball thy claim you can see things, this is evil.
6. A Charmer or Consulter: A wizard, or familiar spirits.
7. A Necromancer: The one who calls up the dead. We are not to call up the dead, you are calling up demonic spirits.

I Samuel 28: 7-19
Saul went unto the Witch at En-dor to call up Samuel to ask him what to do, for he had not heard from God. Saul sealed his death for calling up Samuel. This is very dangerous, the church world has slowly let in these demonic spirits, now they are paying the price, for the church has lost its power and anointing. This is witchcraft spirits, the people are letting this in their homes in form of Televisions, the cartoons the video games. The television is not wrong or games are not wrong if it is pure, Christians beware! These things are abomination unto God there is no

room in your life for these things. This is false **wisdom** and knowledge. God's **Wisdom** is approachable. It is a gift worth seeking for, it gives life not death. When we get wrapped up in these demonic spirits we take on devils (demons) then we need to have them cast out of us. We cannot be a Christian and be possessed, we can be oppressed but not possessed. Demons are not in the Bible there called devils. We need on going flow of **Wisdom**, we must die out the old Adam nature. We are to be in the likeness of the second Adam Jesus Christ.

II Corinthians 5:17
Therefore if any man be in Christ, he is a new creature: old things have passed away; behold (look) all things are become new.
The new creature has become a new person, have no desires for the things of this world. We no longer possess Adam, we took on Jesus Christ.

Ephesians 4:24
And ye put on the new man, which after God is created in righteousness and true holiness.

We are to set our affections on things above, not on earthly desires. I am not saying you cannot go out and do things, but we are to use **Wisdom** where we are to take our children, and monitor what we set before them. I have always said if it is not fit for a child to watch read or play then there is a good chance we should leave it alone as well.

Romans 12:2
And be not conformed to this world; but be ye transformed by the renewing of your mind, that ye may prove what is that good, and acceptable, and perfect will of God.

Conformed (Greek) mold, pattern, fashioned

So we see here we are not to pattern our life after the world, or anyone else. We are to pattern or let God mold us into the perfect man Christ Jesus. We are to be a perfect living sacrifice to give our all which is a reasonable service. God does not want or desire to have a dead sacrifice, he wants lively stones he wants our best, for he gave us his all and his best. We cannot compare the sacrifice he gave to us, but our bodies are the best we can do. We as a believer must possess a single-minded passion to please our Lord and Savior, How? In love, devotion, praise, and holiness unto God. We are to separate ourselves from the world (worldly ways) become a separated people from the world of sin. The sacrifice we are to give is our all, yes my friend Jesus did pay the price on Calvary's Hill the place of the Skull, to crush the enemies head.

Genesis 3:15
And I will put enmity between thee and the woman, and between thy seed and her seed; it shall bruise thy head, and thou shalt bruise his heel.
Bruise (Hebrew) crush, strike, break.

When they place the crown of thorns upon Jesus' head, he crushed or broke the devil's head. Then they drove the nails through the sides of his ankles the place where it broke or crushed the devil's heel. So he is broken, crushed from his head to his feet. Calvary's hill, or Golgotha's Hill is where Jesus was crucified. The side of the hill is a picture formed in the rock of a skull. This is believed to been the very place Adam fell by the tree, and Jesus Died on the tree. As Jesus was crucified on the cross for our sins, and Jesus died, he said take up your cross and follow me. Where did Jesus go? We must take up our cross and follow him. We must go through the fires of hell to be tried as I said earlier. I am not saying literally I am saying spiritually speaking.

Acts 1:8 (Jesus speaking)
"But ye shall receive power after the Holy Ghost is come upon you: and ye shall be witnesses unto me both in Jerusalem, an in all Judea, and in Samaria, and unto the uttermost part of the earth."

- A. In Jerusalem: those who are the closest to you, your inner circle of your family and your closest friends.
- B. In Judea: Those are your circle of friends
- C. Samaria: Those in the outer circle of your friends, mere *acquaintance*
- D. To the end of the earth, strangers, foreigners. Go into all the world and preach the Gospel to every creature. Mark 16:15-16 He that believes and is baptized shall be saved.

We are Empowered with Boldness From on High. He gave us power after the Holy Ghost came. He gave us his power (Holy Ghost) and His name (Jesus). Everything will bow at the name of Jesus.

Those Who Win Souls Are Wise:

We are to open up our bowels of compassion. We are to have a compassion and a love for our fellow man to want to win them to Christ. The love of Jesus Christ is he gave his life so we can live. He loved us so much he took our sins upon his shoulders, 11 Corinthians 5:21;He became sin, who knew no sin. Hebrews 2:9- Came a little lower than the angels; Philippians 2:7-,Came in the form of a servant and to become our sacrifice. Under the law in the Old Testament when time of Passover there were two goats on that was to be sacrificed one who was set free was called the escape goat Leviticus 16:19:30. Then in the New Testament they cried crucify Jesus crucify him set Barabbas free. One had to be set free and one had to die. We were considered a prisoner like Barabbas was. He took our chastisement and our shame and nailed it to the old rugged cross, so that we can have life, and have it more abundantly. We were so unworthy of his love, but by his love and mercy, we are now counted worthy. Do not ever say you are not worthy after you come to the Lord, you are saying Jesus' blood (royal) was not enough to save you to make you worthy. We were not worthy, but by the shedding of his precious blood remits our sins. We open our mouth and let the river of God's power flow through our life, do not dam up the river of life let it flow freely. Look in the medical books the circulatory system where the blood flows throughout all our veins and all our organs is called the River of Life. Life is in the blood. As the body works in the natural it works in the spiritual body as well. God has a body and a many-membered body. Each part of the body has a function and each body part is essential to keep the body in working order.

There are souls to be won, people are dying lost. Time is running out, time is nearing the end. We need to go out to proclaim to the lost and dying world that Jesus loves them. The love of God that abides in us, gives us a love for the sinner, to win them to Christ. We are to love one another as Jesus Christ loves us, and Jesus died for us.

John 15:13
No greater love hath no man than this than to lay down his life for a friend.

I John 4:11
Beloved, if God so loved us, we ought also love one another.

I John 4:8-9
He that loves not, knows not God; for God is LOVE!
9th In this was manifested the love of God toward us, because that God sent his only begotten Son into the World, that we might live through him.
He that believes on the Son shall have life.
Begotten (Greek) only child, unique.

We go out into the world tell them about the love of God, We go to malls, streets, stores, many different places when we are drawn to a person we began talking to them by asking how their day is and they are blessed; and let God lead us in what to say. We must tell them about Jesus Christ and they listen to you then they began to open up.

St Luke 14:23 (Jesus speaking)
"And the Lord said unto the servant. Go out into the highways and hedges, and compel them to come in, that my house may be filled."
Hedges (Greek) country. **Compel** (Greek) force

The Lord wants us to go out in the country, to the gutters, the prisons, the homeless, anywhere there is a sinner we are to go. Now people will not agree here with me but it is true. There are ministers who are called to go to the bars they minister one on one, they are called to where the gangs are like Dave Wilkerson and Nicki Cruse they have that special anointing and calling. The force, I believe it is talking about, is we force our way into where the people are such as gangs and low places to tell them about Jesus and his love. To tell them there is a better way of living and that Jesus loves them as well as anyone else.

To force the Word to go out, everywhere we go. Tell the world that Jesus is the Good Shepherd. He will leave the ninety-nine that are saved; and go out to find that one little lost sheep, to make one-hundred.

John 10:7-9; 27 (Jesus speaking)
"Verily, (Truly) *verily, I say unto you, I am the DOOR of the Sheep!"*
9th *"I AM the DOOR; by me if any man enter, he shall be save, and shall go in and find pasture."*
27th *"My sheep hear my voice, and I know them, and they follow me."*
We have **Wisdom** to know our shepherd's voice, we will not follow another voice. We go in the fold and we find pasture where we eat and are protected from the enemy.

Proverbs 2:7; 10
He lays up sound **Wisdom** for the righteous; he is a buckler to them that walk uprightly.
10th When **Wisdom** enters into thine heart, and knowledge is pleasant unto thy soul.

Proverbs 3:5
Trust in the Lord with all thine heart; and lean not unto thine OWN understanding.

When we lean to our own beliefs we err in the word. Our ways are not God's ways. We are to lean on Jesus, to know his Ways, His ways are established here in the Bible, the inspired Word of God. His thoughts his ways are higher than our ways. When **Wisdom** has entered into our heart we will began to know his ways. We must know His word, the truth will make us free, but we must know his truth first.
Buckler (Hebrew) shield, defense, a leader who protects.

We see here that the Lord is our protector, our shield he is our defense but we must walk uprightly. We are to trust in the Lord in all our ways, lean not to our own self, not our own understanding, not to our own **wisdom** and knowledge for it is sensual and devilish. When we know his ways he shall preserve us, His understanding will keep us in His path. When **Wisdom** enters our heart, our inward man, our motives began to change. Our thought pattern changes, this kind of thoughts will produce good fruit, such as; love, joy, meekness, temperance, longsuffering, peace, gentleness, goodness, faith, Gal.5:22-23

Proverbs 4:10
Hear O My Son, and receive my sayings; and the years of thy life Shall Be MANY!
So the key word here to getting *Wisdom* is to *HEAR!* (Incline!) What the Lord is saying to us, and we shall live in His Presence.

Ecclesiastes 9:18
Wisdom is better than weapons of war: but one sinner destroys much good.

Sow to Your Life the Word of God:

Matthew 13:23
But he that received seed unto good ground is he that hears the Word, and understands it; which also bears fruit, and brings forth some hundredfold, some sixty fold, and some thirty.

II Corinthians 9:6
But this I say, He which sows sparingly shall reap sparingly; and he which sows bountifully shall reap bountifully.

We must not stop anywhere in our Christian walk with the Lord Apostle Paul said this is a pressing way. We are to keep pressing forward never to set down and wait to die. We must constantly study, read, to pray, if we do not we will wither away and die as a seed that is planted needs water and sunshine. When we plant in the spring we are to plant bountiful, we will reap plenty, we are rewarded at the end of harvest just what we sown. I planted a flower garden one year I planted marigolds and several kinds of other flowers, but when the harvest time came I picked a marigold, I opened up the flower I counted 36 seeds from one seed I had planted. My, My! Look what transpired from one little tiny seed. When we sow one Word in the field, we are planting and reaping souls into the Kingdom. We must sow different seed also. We sow the Word and we sow money. We sow different ways but we must sow in all areas. We must sow good seed in the garden of our heart, we must weed our garden, to choke out any weeds that try to grow. How do we do this? By studying the Bible and through praying, and through fasting. If we do not pull the weeds it will choke out the good seeds and discord is sown in its place. We surely do not want to reap discord and strife.

Let us go back to the Book of Proverbs 11:1
A FALSE BALANCE! Is an abomination to the Lord, but a just weight is his delight.
Abomination (Hebrew) detestable, loathsome.

Three is the balance:

Three is the balance all through the Bible three is resurrection and life, same as seven, perfection. Three and seven go hand in hand all through the Bible. There is the Three major Feasts with seven; intertwined in the three feast. There is three throughout the Bible, I can give you more examples here: There is The Father,

Son, The Holy Ghost: The Word, the Name, The blood; **Wisdom**, Knowledge and Understanding; Cannot have one without the other or it becomes out of balance. We are releasing the *Wisdom* of God in our lives, and it is pleasant to the soul. The righteous is delivered out of trouble, righteous living brings an abundance of harvest and life to our soul. This does not mean we do not suffer, we learn through our sufferings, just as Jesus learned by the things he suffered. When the field is planted, there is more than just sunshine, there is the hot scorching sun, there is the rains the storms but through it all comes harvest these elements brought forth full fruit in harvest.

Meditate On the Word:

What does it mean to Meditate on the Word of God? To think about, to practice. To dwell on the goodness of His promises. When we practice, we make perfect. To think of his word to memorize it put in in our heart. When we read the Word we get on our mind, the word become life to us. The word is like a wellspring springing up into everlasting Joy. The well spring of joy in our everyday lives bubbles up and over like an Artesian Well. We become like a tree planted deep by the river of life. As a strong tree produces good luscious fruit; we will produce good mature luscious fruit.

Abraham Chose God's Way:

Genesis 12:1-3
Now the Lord has said unto Abram, get thee out of thy country, and from thy kindred, and from thy father's house, unto a land that I will show thee,
2nd And make thee a great nation, and I will bless thee, and make thy name great; and thou shalt be a blessing

3rd And I will bless them that bless thee, and curse them that curse thee: and in thee shall all the families of the earth be blessed.

We see here where by faith Abram knew he heard from God; there is a knowing, an assurance that you know. You cannot explain it, but you know when you hear a divine call of God. You see here God told Abram to go but did not tell him how far, he was to go and keep his ear (inclined) open to know when to stop. What great **Wisdom** and such faith to know you heard, but you only know to go till he tells him to stop. He had the **Wisdom** to know he heard, he had the knowledge to pack up and go, he had the understanding he had to leave his father's house. There is surely a balance here. Abram came from the lineage of Shem, Noah's son, Abram's father was Terah. Abram was 75 years old when he left Haran, he took Sarai his wife and his nephew, Lot.

Genesis 15:1-2
After these things the word of the Lord came unto Abram in a vision, saying Fear not, Abram; I AM thy shield and thy exceeding great reward.
And Abram said, Lord God, what wilt thou give me, seeing I go childless, and the steward of my house is this Eliezer of Damascus.

Genesis 17:1-13
And Abram was ninety years old and nine, the Lord appeared to Abram, and said unto him, I am the Almighty God; walk before me, and be thou perfect.
5th Neither shall thy name any more be called Abram, but thy name shall be called ABRAHAM; for a father of many nations have I made thee.

6th And I will make the exceeding fruitful, and make nations of thee, and kings shall come out of thee.

Genesis 21: 5
And Abraham was a hundred years old, when his son Isaac was born unto him.

Genesis 22:1:14
And it came to pass after these things, that God did tempt (tested) Abraham, and said unto him, Abraham; and he said, Behold, here I am.
2nd And he said, Take now thy son, thine only son Isaac, whom thou lovest, and get thee into the land of Moriah; and offer him there for a burnt offering upon one of the mountains which I tell thee of.
4th Then on the THIRD (three) Day Abraham lifted up his eyes and saw the place afar off.
5th And Abraham said unto his young men, abide ye here with the ass; and I and the lad will go yonder and worship, and come again to you.
6th And Abraham took the wood of the burnt offering; and laid it upon Isaac his son; and he took the fire in his hand, and a knife; and they went both of them together.
8th And Abraham said, my son, God will provide himself lamb for the burnt offering; so they went both of them together.
10th And Abraham stretched forth his hand, and took the knife to slay is son.
11th And the angel of the Lord called unto him out of heaven, and said Abraham, Abraham, and he said here am I.
12th And he said lay not thine hand upon the lad.
13th And Abraham lifted up his eyes and looked, and behold behind him was a ram caught in a thicket by his horns: And

Abraham went and took the ram and offered him up for a burnt offering instead of his son.

Abraham Take your only son Isaac, outside to the land Moriah verse 2, God gave his only begotten son; John 3:16-Mt. Moriah at the time of Abraham is believed to be in Jerusalem where Jesus was crucified outside the city. Isaac carried his own wood upon himself, verse six, Jesus carried the cross. John 19:17; Where is the Lamb for the burnt offering Isaac asked 7th and 8th verse; John 1:29; John sees Jesus! Behold the Lamb of God who takes away the sin of the world. A three day journey Abraham went to take his son Isaac, Jesus rose on the third day. By faith Abraham when he was tried, offered up Isaac; and he had received the promises offered up his only son Hebrews 11:17; Abraham gave his only son by Sarah, God gave his only Son Jesus Christ.

Can we see the New Testament concealed in the Old Testament? We see **Wisdom** at work here, to see the finished work of Calvary.

Hebrews 11:31
By faith the harlot Rahab perished not with them that believed not, when she had received the spies with peace.

Rahab when she saw the spies she knew by faith to hide them: to protect them from her people. By **Wisdom** she saved herself and her household. But her family had to be in her household in order to be saved.

James 2:24-Likewise also was not Rahab the harlot justified by works, when she had received the messengers, and had sent them out another way?

Joshua 2:4, 15-22
And the woman took the two men, and hid them, and said thus. There came men unto me, but I wist not whense they were.
15th then she let them down by a cord through the window; for her house was upon the town wall, and she dwelt upon the wall.
21st And she said according unto your words, so be it. And she sent them away, and they departed: and she bound the scarlet line in the window.
22; And they went, and came to the mountain, and abode there three days until the pursuers were returned; and the pursuers sought them throughout all the way but found them not.

As we see here Joshua sent out two spies to spy out the land. The two men were spotted they knew the two men went into the harlot Rahab's house. Rahab took the two men and hid them on her roof top under the stalks of flax (linen) she laid in order upon her roof. The scarlet cord: the color scarlet is made of two colors, red and purple. Purple was very expensive to make, only the people of royalty wore purple for that reason. Purple means royalty. Red represents the blood and the atonement of our salvation. The cord served several purposes, it had to be strong, to hold two men, to be long to reach the ground. As she hung the cord out the window she saved her and her household. She married Salmon they had a son named Boaz who married Ruth.

Ruth 1:6-8,14, 16-17
The she arose with her daughters-in-law, that she might return from the country of Moab: for she had heard in the country of Moab how that the Lord had visited his people in giving them bread.
8th And Naomi said unto her two daughters-in-law, Go, return each other to her mother's house; The Lord deal kindly with you, as ye have dealt with the dead, and with me.

14th And they lifted up their voices and wept again; and Orpah kissed her mother-in-law; but Ruth clave unto her.
16th And Ruth said, Intreat me not to leave thee, or return from following after; for whither thou goest I will go; and where thou lodges I will lodge; thy people shall by my people, and thy God my God.

Ruth 1:22
So Naomi returned, and Ruth the Moabitess, her daughter-in-law, with her, which returned out of the country of Moab: and they came to Bethlehem in the beginning of the harvest (fall).

We see a young woman who lost her husband through death, she had no children by her husband. She loved her mother-in-law, she had a bond with her. Ruth loved her as her own mother. She would not stay behind with her family and let Naomi leave without her. Ruth clave unto her told her, please do not tell me to go back to my family do not tell me to go back, I will stand by you, go where you go, Serve the same God you serve. Nothing would persuade Ruth to stay behind, to watch her much loved mother-in-law leave her behind she was persistent.

Ruth 2:1-8
And Noami had a kinsman of her husband's a mighty man of wealth, of the family of Elimelech; and his name was Boaz.
2nd And Ruth the Moabitess said unto Naomi, let me now go to the field, and glean ears of corn after him in whose sight I shall find GRACE. And she said unto her Go my daughter.
8th Then said Boaz unto Ruth, Hear thou not, my daughter? Go not to glean in another field, neither go from thence, but abide here fast by my maidens

Ruth 3:1-15
Then Naomi her mother-in-law said unto her, My daughter shall I not seek rest for thee, that it may be well with thee.
2nd And now is not Boaz of our kindred, with whose maidens thou wast? Behold, he winnoweth barley to night in the threshing-floor (barn-floor)
Winnoweth (Hebrew) to spread out, to measure off,

Matthew 3:12
Whose fan is in his hand, and he will thoroughly purge his floor, and gather his wheat into the garner; but he will burn up the chaff and unquenchable fire.
Fan (Greek) shovel, pitch fork.
Purge (Greek) to clear out, clean out, thoroughly.
Garner (Greek) storehouse.

The Lord will take a shovel clear out and thoroughly clean his floor to take a pitchfork to gather his wheat into the storehouse. We represent the wheat his is purging taking through the unquenchable fires to make us pure and clean.

Boaz was a type of Jesus Christ, and Ruth portrays the Bride (The name Ruth means a friend). Ruth was a Moabite, from the tribe of Lot and his daughters. Ruth was a Gentile! ("Oh no") Boaz was a Jew. How can that be? God had to come through both the Gentles and to the Jews in order to graft in the Gentiles to make one new man. Boaz was second in line, to redeem Ruth, he had to go to the next of kin.

Ruth 4:1-6
Then went Boaz up to the gate, and sat him down there; and behold, (look) the kinsman of whom Boaz spoke came by; unto

whom he said, Ho, such a one! Turn aside, sit down here. And he turned aside, and set down.

6th And the kinsman said, I cannot redeem it for myself, lest I mare mine own inheritance: redeem thou my right to myself; for I cannot redeem it.

The first Adam could not redeem us, the second Adam which is Jesus Christ came to redeem back the Bride, redeem means to purchase back, to ransom, deliver. Naomi gave Ruth instructions on what she must do, Ruth listened intently. Naomi had two brother's-in-laws, the first brother-in-law could not redeem or purchase Ruth he had already obligated himself. The second one was Boaz, He was next in line and he could redeem her, to purchase Ruth. What do you mean to buy a wife? Back in the Old Testament the bride had to be purchased. When Jesus came to die for us to redeem back or make a purchase we were bought with a price. Boaz represented Jesus Christ, the bridegroom the Jew. Ruth represents the Bride of Christ the Moabite the bride has to be bought, to be redeemed back to God, he had to come through it all to redeem it all back to him to bring the division of two into one new man. God never had to purchase anything but one thing that was man, by and through the blood of the Lamb.

Jesus Before The Cross:

Isaiah 53:3
He was despised and rejected of men, a man of sorrows, and acquainted with grief; and we hid as it were our faces from him; he was despised, and we esteemed him not.

All that Jesus did in his earthly ministry and Calvary would have been to no avail if it were not for what Jesus is doing today. Very little is being preached of what he is doing today. He not only died on a cruel cross of Calvary took our sins nailing them to the cross, it is also what he is doing right now.

The Present Day Ministry of Jesus Christ

Mediator:

I Timothy 2:5
For there is One God, and **One Mediator** (A Go Between) between God and men, the man Christ Jesus.

Jesus is a one time Mediator between God and man. You can only be born natural one time, you can only be born again in the spirit one time. You cannot be unborn, in the natural as well as the spiritual.

You can only be saved once, not multiple times. Man could not approach God in his condition of spiritual death.

Ephesians 4:24
And that ye put on one new man, which after God is created in righteousness and true holiness.
Jesus going to the cross to redeem man back to himself made man approachable to God through Christ.

Advocate: counselor, comforter, helper, intercessor, refers to the Holy Ghost and Jesus Christ.

I John 2:1-2
My little children, these things write I unto you, that ye **SIN NOT**. And **IF** any man sin, we have an Advocate with the Father, Jesus Christ the righteous;
2nd And he is the propitiation for our sins, and not for ours only, but also for the sins of the WHOLE WORLD!
We went through the Mediator when we are born again, then after that, Jesus becomes our Advocate. The Lord said if we sin

to have an advocate with the Father, in other words he becomes our counselor our help in time of trouble, he intercedes for us.
Intercessor: petition, to intercede, to deal with, appeal.

Hebrews 7: 25
Wherefore he is able also to save them to the uttermost that come unto God by him, seeing he ever lives to make intercession for them.
He is our intercessor, he interceded for us, he made his appeal for us, he dealt with it on the cross, nailing it once and for all. He made our petition known unto God. We see here Jesus is the Mediator for the sinners, But then he is the Intercessor for the Christians.

Romans 12:2
And be not conformed to this world; but be ye transformed by the renewing of your mind, that ye prove what is good and acceptable and perfect will of God.
Conformed (Greek) to pattern, mold, to fashion.
Transformed (Greek) changed, transfigured.
We are not to be patterned or molded after the worldly ways of man; but we are to be changed to have a new mind set so that we can know the mind of Jesus Christ. To be in the Father's perfect (mature) will. He is able to save us to the uttermost.

The High Priest:

Hebrews 5:1-5
For every high priest taken from among men is ordained for men in things pertaining to God, that he may offer both gifts and sacrifices for sins.
2nd Who can have compassion on the ignorant, and on them that are out of the way; for that he himself also is compassed with infirmities.

5ᵗʰ So also Christ glorified not himself to be made an high priest; but he that said unto him, Thou art my Son, today have I begotten thee.

Jesus was the ultimate and last sacrifice to be offered, the last blood to be shed and placed upon the Mercy seat for our atonement, through the sacrifice was offered gifts to many the first gift offered was the gift of salvation to mankind. God had compassion on us being ignorant in our sins. He healed our sin sicknesses through his stripes upon his back. Jesus was made the Great High Priest, to go into the Holy of Holies, we are the Holy of Holies where the Great High Priest Dwells, he applied the blood to the door post of our heart, He said where he is there we may be also. He took up his abode in us the day we had took him as our Mediator between God and man, then he became our Intercessor we can talk to him on a personal basis, for he made a way through him being our great High Priest.

Romans 5:2
By whom also we have access by faith into grace wherein we **stand,** and rejoice in hope of the glory of God.

11 Thessalonians 2:15
Therefore, brethren, **Stand** fast, and hold the traditions which ye have been taught, whether by word, or our epistle.
Fast (Greek) to stand firm, to be steadfast.

We are to stand firm, to be unmovable; to hold on to the true Word which you have been taught by the Holy Ghost or Epistle (letter).

Acts 7:51-60

Ye stiff-necked and uncircumcised in heart and ears, ye do always resist the Holy Ghost: as your fathers did, so do ye.

52nd Which of the prophets have not your fathers persecuted? And they have slain them showed before of the coming of the Just One: Of whom ye have been now the betrayers and murderers;

58th And cast him out of the city, and stoned him: and the witnesses laid down their clothes at a young man's feet, whose name was Saul.

59th And they stoned Stephen, calling upon God, and saying, Lord Jesus, receive my spirit.

Stiff-necked (Greek) Stubborn, to be hardened, the hardness of heart.

Uncircumcised (Greek) possibly of being stubborn. Not circumcised.

Acts 6:3-15

Wherefore, brethren, look ye out among you seven (perfection, completion) men of honest report, full of the Holy Ghost and **Wisdom**, whom we may appoint over this business.

5th And the saying pleased the whole multitude: and they chose Stephen, a man full of faith and of the Holy Ghost, and Philip and Prochorus, and Nicanor, and Timon, and Parmenas, and Nicolas a proselyte of Antioch;

6th Whom they set before the Apostles; and when they prayed, they laid their hands on them.

8th And Stephen full of faith and power, did great wonders and miracles among the people.

15th And all that sat in the counsel, looking steadfastly on him, saw his face as it had been the face of an angel.

Colossians 1:10
That you might walk worthy of the Lord unto all pleasing, being fruitful in good work, and increasing in the knowledge of God.

We are to walk worthy in everything we do in word or deed. Not to let our work be in vain or to have our work to be evil spoken of. Sometimes this is impossible, for people will let the devil take control of their tongue to be used of the devil. We are not too loose faith or hope; when the enemy comes knocking just remember; God says in his word; when the enemy comes in like a flood, God will raise up a standard against him. We must stand strong, to grow in the knowledge of God, by studying the Bible daily, such as; the Bible devotions "Daily Bread" for it is food for our soul. When we know the Word that is more weapons we can use to bind up the enemy when he come roaring "Like" A Lion.

Colossians 3:17
And whatever ye do in word or deed, do all in the name of the Lord Jesus Christ, giving thanks to God and the Father by him.

Colossians 4:5
Walk in **WISDOM** toward them that are without, redeeming the time.
Redeeming (Greek) to make the most of the time. The act of purchasing something in the market place.

Let us walk in the power of His might, to walk in **Wisdom** for **Wisdom** is wise in all she does. She builds her house with love, she keeps her family for they are never in want. We are to never waste time for it is valuable. **Wisdom** is far above rubies, she is priceless. **Wisdom** gives instruction to the one who desires knowledge. A fool cannot obtain **Wisdom** for **Wisdom** is too high for a fool. **Wisdom** is clothed in strength, and in honor. When she opens her mouth she is kind she looks to her household she takes care of her children, and to all that is around her.

II Timothy 2:19
Nevertheless the foundation of God stands sure, having this seal. The Lord knows them that are his. And let everyone that is named the name of Christ depart from iniquity. Iniquity - Greek: wrong doing, evil, unjust

We must stand on the foundation of God. The foundation is; the Chief Corner Stone, which is Jesus Christ. Jesus told Peter in Matthew

Matthew 16:18-19
And I say unto thee, That thou art Peter, and Upon this Rock I will build my church and the gates of hell shall not prevail against it.
19th And I will give unto thee the keys of the kingdom of heaven.

Jesus Christ is the Rock, He is Rock of Age of offense, he gives us the keys of his kingdom. 1 Peter 2:6-8. For when we stumble and fall he is there to pick us up. We were in sin which is a stumbling block or an obstacle that separates us from the Lord. When we come to the Lord we repent of our sins the stumbling block is removed for the Lord is our Rock of Offence. So with Jesus in our hearts we are saved from iniquity. Iniquity is; wickedness, evil doing, unrighteousness, doing any wrong doing, anything that will keep us from the righteousness of God.

I Corinthians 2:4-5
And my speech and my preaching was not with enticing words of man's **Wisdom**, but in demonstration of the spirit of power.

5th That your faith should not Stand in the **Wisdom** of men, but in the power of God.

Paul was a man of great intelligence. He was a very educated man, he was highly esteemed in the Roman history books. Paul was not only a lawyer, Acts 22:3; he was thought to be of the Sanhedrin Counsel: which is made up of the Sadducees which made up of the majority, the Pharisees which made up of the minority. The scribes which is also means lawyer, this made up "the court of seventy one men." So why I brought this out is to see where Apostle Paul is coming from. He was a man of great influence and prestige. Paul was highly educated of the finest quality of schools, with great worldly **wisdom**. This is why he said what he said; I come not with enticing words of man's **wisdom**, but in the demonstration of the spirit of power. He was saying He came under the guidance of the Holy Ghost, not by his education of men. The Holy Ghost is a great teacher.

Isaiah 33:6
And **Wisdom** and knowledge shall be the stability of thy times, and strength of salvation: the fear of the Lord is his treasure.

I Corinthians 2:13-16
Which things also we speak, not in words which man's **Wisdom** teaches, but which the Holy Ghost teaches; comparing spiritual things with spiritual.
14th But the natural man receives not the things of the spirit of God: for they are foolishness unto him; neither can he know them, because they are spiritually discerned.

We will see here as we compare to Apostle Paul before his conversion, how he was a natural man, what we call a carnal man. Before his conversion according to Acts 9:18; he was called Saul of Tarsus, Saul was a very carnal man, he destroyed everything in his path that had to do with Jesus Christ for he was still operating under the old law. He had men and women put to death that was a Christian thinking he was doing a just thing. When he was struck down on the Road to Damascus and he was blinded, God spoke to Saul. Acts 9:4; He asked Saul; why persecuted thou me? Saul relied on his teaching of the law, he could not discern the spiritual things for they are spiritually discerned. Then when God struck him down and blinded him then he began to see even though he was blind. God changed his name for he was no longer the same. His name was changed to Paul. God raised him up to be the greatest Apostle known to man. Apostle Paul wrote over half of the New Testament. Paul was no longer carnal, the ***wisdom*** Paul had God changed him to show him his **Wisdom** from above is pure, to show him we are no longer under the old law. Jesus fulfilled the law, now we are now under a New Covenant called **GRACE!**

16th For who hath the mind of the Lord, that he may instruct him? But we have the mind of Christ.

We must put on the mind of Christ, to walk in **Wisdom**, in the power and demonstration of the Holy Ghost. Paul had the same **wisdom**,but when God changed him, the law (the letter),the **Wisdom** changed to Grace, and it brought life not death, to have the knowledge of his Word, which brings understanding through **Wisdom**. It is no longer I that lives it is the Christ in me. **Wisdom** instructs us what to do, how to stand, when to speak, and how to speak. It even changes how we walk, the countenance on our faces change, it has a glow of the Holy Ghost.

I Peter 5:12
By Silvanus, a faithful witness brother unto you, as I suppose, I have written briefly, exhorting, and testifying that this is the true Grace of God wherein ye **stand**.

There are so many more scriptures on how to stand on the **Wisdom** of God, to glean from his Word. We see here where there is a difference in worldly **wisdom** verses the spiritual **Wisdom**. We by faith *stand* on the **Wisdom** of God.

Notes

Chapter 7

How to Grow and Increase in the Knowledge of God

II Peter 3:18
But grow in Grace, and in the knowledge of our God and Savior Jesus Christ. To him be glory both now and forever. Amen.

Ephesians 4:15
But speaking the truth in love, may grow up into him in all things, which is the head, even Christ

II Timothy 1:7
For God has not given us a spirit of fear; but of power, and of love, and of a sound mind.

The Lord desires us to grow up in his Grace and in his knowledge, not in the knowledge and traditions of men but in God Almighty. Speak the truth of his love, growing up into him with us being his body, and him the head. God does not want us to have fear of men, he wants us to walk in the power of his might. To have a sound mind to have our mind stayed on him, in other words fixed on the Lord.

Colossians 4:2
Continue in prayer, watch in the same thanksgiving.

Let your speech be always in Grace, to be seasoned with salt, that ye may know how ye ought to answer every man.

Ephesians 6:10
Finally my brethren, be strong in the Lord, and in the power of his might.
11th Put on the whole armor of God, that ye be able to stand against the wiles (tricks scheming) of the devil.

We cannot go to war without first going to boot-camp we must first learn the strategies of the enemy and his scheming ways in which he operates. We must prepare for battle, how? By studying.

II Timothy 2:15
Study to show thyself approved unto God a workman that need not to be ashamed rightly dividing the word of truth. Ephesians 6:11-18 tells us we are to put on the whole armor of God, so that we can stand against to tricks of the Devil. We must learn how to pray, it is the most effective tool we have. We are to pray the word according to our circumstances, just as Jesus did when he went into the wilderness to be tempted of the devil. If we do not communicate how can we have a relationship with the Lord? We are to know how the Lord operates in the knowledge with understanding. **Wisdom** brings a knowing how to operate and when to move in the spirit. God has given us weapons of warfare and it will cost you your life if you are not prepared for battle. Our weapons are not carnal. We are fighting a war between good and evil. We must stay teachable, not one person knows it all, it takes the whole body joined together to teach one another.

Matthew 4:1-11

The Jesus was led up of the spirit into the wilderness to be tempted of the devil.

2nd And when he had fasted forty days and forty nights, he was afterward an hungered.

9th And said unto him, ALL things will I give thee, if thou will fall down and worship me.

10th Then said Jesus unto him, (Jesus speaking) *"Get thee hence, Satan: for it is written, Thou shalt worship the Lord thy God, and him only shalt thou serve."*

11th Then the devil leaves him, and behold angels came and ministered unto him.

The Lord gave us the greatest illustration to us here on how to overcome the enemy. This is a warfare going on here. This is the battlefield of the mind. The devil came to temp Jesus three times here in these ten verses. Jesus was tempted, he was hungry, then enemy came in like a flood, tempting him with food, I believe Jesus being hungry was really tempted, but through his praying with his fasting when He spoke the Word of God to him the devil no doubt left him. Then the devil returns with another strategy to tempt Jesus. 5th v. He took Jesus up into the holy city sets him on a pinnacle (highest point) of the temple. The devil told him if he was the Son of God, then cast thyself down; He shall give his angels charge concerning thee: and in their hands they shall bear thee up, lest at any time thou dash thy foot against a stone. The Devil quotes Psalms 91:11; the devil distorted the word of God, he only gives part truths. 7th v. Jesus said unto him, *"It is written again,* (Jesus speaking) *Thou shalt not temp the Lord thy God."* Matthew 22:29; Jesus answered and said unto them, (Jesus speaking) *Ye do err, not knowing the scriptures, nor the power of God."* 8th v. Again the devil takes him up into an exceeding high mountain, and shows him all the kingdoms of the world, and the glory of them 9th v. And said unto him, all these things will I give thee, if thou will fall down and worship me. 10th v. Then Jesus said unto him, (Jesus speaking) *"Get Thee hence, (away) Satan; for it is written, Thou shalt worship the Lord thy God, and him only shalt thou serve."* Well how can the devil give to Jesus something he does not have? Why would Jesus bow down and worship his enemy. But here we see each of the three times that the devil came to tempt Jesus, Jesus had a word for to put the devil under his feet. Then when the fasting of forty was over the angels came to minister unto him. What I am saying here we must know the Word for the Word to be able to set us free of the temptation and trials we are facing at the time.

We see here so plain there are the three major sins: The devil came at Jesus the same way he did Eve. The lust of the flesh, lust of the eyes, the pride of life. But Jesus gave him the devil the truth, for he said IT IS WRITTEN! The WORD he spoke, and the devil had to flee.

II Corinthians 10
(For the weapons of our warfare are not carnal, but mighty through God to the pulling down of stronghold).

We see here we are not fighting a natural war, we are fighting against principalities, against powers of darkness against spiritual wickedness in high places. One of the high places is our fleshly mind warring after the spirit.

We must welcome discipline, be honest, and obedient to God. Walk in the spirit, walk in his **Wisdom**, we must have a vision, or we will perish, Why is that? We have dreams, we have visions this is what keeps us pressing on. When we have no visions or dreams, we have no hope, we have given up. The discipline that we go through keeps us wise, keep us humble.

Proverbs 4:5-6 &18
Get **Wisdom,** get understanding, forget it not; neither decline from the words of thy mouth.
6th Forsake her not, and she shall preserve thee: love her and she shall keep thee.
18th But the path of the just is as the shining light, that shines more and more unto the perfect day.

The perfect day is the seventh day which means The Lord rested on the seventh day; for The Lord is our rest. The Lord is our light; he is our rest, our peace, our shelter in the time of the storms.
Decline (Hebrew) turn away

Remember **Wisdom** is the principle thing. She will keep you in the path of righteousness. The path of righteousness is the dawning of light that shines more and more unto the perfect day.
Principle (Hebrew) what is first, beginning, first-fruit. Chiefest.
So we see here that **Wisdom** is the first and foremost in our lives. **Wisdom** is the first thing and the chiefest.

Proverbs 4:23
The heart will be kept with all diligence; for out of it are the issues of life.
Diligence (Hebrew) guard or guarding, watch, custody.

As we guard our heart and also take care of our heart, to allow the Lord Jesus to rule and reign in our heart, he will take care of the issues of our heart if we give him complete control.

God's Wisdom is Gentle:

James 3:17
But the **Wisdom** that is from above is first pure, then peaceable, gentle, and easy to be intreated, full of mercy and good fruits, without partiality, without hypocrisy.
Intreated (Greek) submissive, obedient, compliant.
Wisdom is easy to become submissive to, to become obedient with all diligence. Then we will bear good fruit without partiality and showing pride or being boastful.
Hypocrisy (Greek) Pride-full show.

As we see here in the book of James, **Wisdom** is first pure, then it is peaceable, it brings peace within us first then to our brethren, we are to have mercy one to another, to love with all diligence. We must bear good fruit, when we are in line of the spirit and in word and in deed we will bear good fruit. Good fruit will become natural in our walk with the lord.
Pure (Greek) innocent, chaste, clear, sincerely.

Wisdom is first innocent, she is sincere in all her ways. **Wisdom** brings peace in all she does, she is compliant she is submissive, she shows no pride for she is humble. **Wisdom** is approachable she shows love and mercy everywhere she goes. This is why we can approach God, His Grace and Mercy made him approachable.

We cannot have envy and strife along with peace, and love, it does not mix. This kind of attitude will bring confusion and hurt in the body of Christ. Confusion and strife is not of God, it is devilish. We are to keep our focus on the Lord, to seek his way not our way. **Wisdom** is, first pure, then she brings peace that passes all understanding in our heart, she is gentle, not hostile it brings us to be merciful and allows us to produce good fruit.

Self-pity is not what we need, it is strength we need in the time of trouble; in the time of our storm. Self-pity gets us nowhere fast. We are to stand on God's promises, on the power of God. We must learn to praise him in the midst of our storms literally and spiritually. Why praise? When we raise our hands in the air we are surrendering to God, this confuses the enemy also. Praise also takes us into to the realm of worship. This is where healing takes place, this is where the victory begins, this giving full control over to God. As the disciples were in the boat a storm suddenly arose, the disciples panicked, they cried "WE are going to Die!" They did not even think to act on their faith, neither did they use **Wisdom** nor the knowledge of the situation to save themselves in the midst of the storm, they were too scared. The disciples acted out of fear not on faith. Jesus was asleep in the boat as the storm was raging high. The disciples cried out in a panic; "Lord wake up!" Save us or we parish! The Lord woke stood up with power and authority; He spoke to the wind to calm down and the wind obeyed. What man is this that the winds obey? Jesus asked His disciples; why they were so afraid? Where is your faith? This to show us we must have faith to speak with power and authority or we will drown in our storms of life.

The weapons that come against us cannot prosper, they cannot overpower us, or defeat us. When the storms of life are raging high at its very peak, we are at the threshold of a breakthrough, but just at the brink of a miracle some people quit, or complain and detain their breakthrough. If we stand still, wait, and listen, the Lord will bring us through. There is an old saying here; "If God takes us to it, he will bring us through it." So many times we under estimate the power of God. When we panic we do not have the situation under control. In times of panic we do not reason or do anything we are taught to do, we do not use **Wisdom** in the situation we are in, or the knowledge of the situation. We run around like a chicken with his head cut off, as the old saying goes. Many times we in the boat of life and the storms hit with no warning that sends us railing back and forth as a flag in a wind storm. We are to use the power tools the Lord gave us, **The Word, Blood and the Name**. We are covered by and through His blood, we took on His Name, which gave us his power, The Word, Which we use when the enemy come in like a flood. Each storm of life makes us stronger, gives us experience, each mountain we climb gives us strength also, we find just the smallest edge to grab ahold of to pull us up, we must never look down or we will lose our focus and our grip of life. We must go through life's lessons this is what matures us for the next lesson of life. When we start school we do not start at grade twelve, we start at kindergarten level. We must learn the basics of life a level at a time. This is the way of life's lessons it teaches us step by step, level by level till we graduated from high school, we have learned the **Wisdom** and knowledge of life, and we have an understanding of what we have learned. Now there is college and it goes on to a faster learning, in college, what took nine months in school takes around eight to twelve weeks to learn. This is the way it is in our walk with God, we learn all the time, we will always have trials, mountains, deserts, valleys in our Christian walk, each one gets harder, but one thing for certain we want to praise the Lord and not to complain as the children of Israel did or we will find ourselves walking around that same mountain, we do not want to walk around it we need to climb the mountain to get to the other side to find a new valley a new mountain. For every Mountain we climb there is a valley before us, the mountain is getting us ready for the valley ahead. The word we are to put in our heart that we will not sin against God, the more word we know, the more we can stand against the tricks of the devil, the more we grow up in the Lord. We must learn to obey, to praise the Lord through the most trying times, this brings victory. God inhabits the praise of his people; he desires to hear from us daily. How do we learn to praise the Lord? In our trials and while going through deserts. We speak the Word through our circumstances of life. This is why we must know the word, for the word makes us free from the enemy's clutches.

I Samuel 17:38-54
And Saul armed David with his armor, put on a helmet of brass () upon his head; also he armed him with a coat of mail.
39th And David girded his sword upon his armor, and he assayed to go; for he had not proved it. And David said unto Saul, I cannot go with these; for I have not proved them. And David put them off.
40th And he took his staff in his hand, and chose him five (grace) smooth stones out of the brook, and put them in a shepherd's bag which he had, even in a scrip; and his sling was in his hand; and he drew near to the Philistine.
Assayed (Hebrew) to begin, determined, willingly.
Mail (Hebrew) scales **(as on skin of a marine creatures)** scale armor.
Scrip (Hebrew) pouch.

We see here a great lesson to glean on: Saul gave David his armor, his weapons of warfare. David tried it on and it did not fit, it was too big. David threw it off, took his sling and his stones and with his shepherd staff in hand. What took place here: when David put on Saul's armor he put on the traditions of men the old Adam nature. Then he shook off the old Adam nature and he put on the Armor of God. He went to Goliath the Philistine. Can you imagine David small in stature facing a nine to ten foot giant? I can hear the giant roaring in laughter, then he said to David; come to me I will give your flesh to the fowls of the air, David did not back down, he did not look in the natural or he would have coward down, but he looked in the spirit, he stood straight he looked Goliath straight in the eyes and spoke in the power of the Lord. He prophesied I will kill you, I will cut off your head, feed your carcass to the fowls of the air and the beasts of the earth. What I am saying here; Saul represents the old Adam nature, our fleshly ways of man. Saul had David to put on his armor which did not fit, but Saul still pressed him to wear it anyway, for that was the only armor Saul had known. David put on the armor thinking it was the right thing to do, but it was too big, it did not fit properly. Saul did not realize he had put his people in great danger for if David lost the battle they would be slaves to the Philistines. David used **Wisdom** here knowing he had to throw off the armor and go in the name of the Lord. We must prophesy to our giants in life, we must stand still, throw our head up high stand like flint, throw off the traditions of men, the old Adam nature, and put on the second Adam which Is Jesus Christ. We have authority to speak to our enemy we do not have to wait on the Lord for he gave us power over the enemy, if we tread on serpents, or drink any deadly poison we are protected under the blood. The Lord abides in us we abide in him ask what we will, we under estimate the power of God within us. So let us go to battle in the name of the Lord.

David's First Anointing: Prophet - Training for reigning:

David was anointed here as a prophet, in the midst of his brethren, David being the eighth child of Jesse, which eight means new beginnings. A prophet is a not only a minister of the Word he is the eyes of the church. A person that prophesies does not mean he/she is a prophet, but a prophet must prophesy. They are also a teacher, a seer, God reveals his word first to his Prophet and Apostle, Ephesians 3:5

I Samuel 16:1:13

And the Lord said unto Samuel, How long wilt thou mourn for Saul, seeing I have rejected him from reigning over Israel? Fill thine horn with oil, and go, I will send thee to Jesse the Bethlehemite: for I have provided me a king among his sons.

7th But the Lord said unto Samuel, Look not on his countenance, or on his height of his stature: because I have refused him; for the Lord sees not as man sees: for the man looks on the outward appearance, but the Lord looks on the Heart.

10th Again, Jesse made seven (Perfection, completion, maturity) sons to pass before Samuel. And Samuel said unto Jesse, The Lord had not Chosen these.

11th And Samuel said unto Jesse, Are here all thy children? And he said, there remains yet the youngest, and behold, he keeps the sheep. And Samuel said unto Jesse, Send and fetch him; for we will not set down till he comes hither.

12th And he sent, and brought him in, now he was ruddy, (red) and withal of a beautiful countenance and goodly to look to, And the Lord said, Arise, anoint him: for this is he.

13th Then Samuel took the horn of oil, and anointed him in midst of his brethren ; and the spirit of the Lord came upon David from the day forward, so Samuel rose up, and went to Ramah.

We see here where it looked like Jesse did not recognize his youngest son, He did not want him to be recognized nor did he feel he was the one to be chosen. Jesse did not realize when he taught David to take care of his sheep to be a shepherd of his flock he had his son David in training for reigning. David being a shepherd boy he did not realize he was in training, for reigning. He was in the pasture taking care of sheep, protecting them, a true shepherd protects his sheep with his life. The shepherd acts as a door across the fold. The enemy has to go through the door to get to the sheep, David slew a bear, and a lion.

The Second Anointing: Priest/King-The ministry of Reigning and Ruling! King

The second anointing is David, King over the house of Judah (praise) shadowed forth the Lord Jesus as King. David took Judah. The first anointing did not make him king, it made him a prophet to become a King in God's appointed time. David was king over the house of Judah for 7 ½ years. - 11 Samuel 2:4;

The Third Anointing: King - David as King of All Israel

David captures Zion. But you see where he had to first become King over Judah, (Lion's whelp) do you see just because Samuel went to the house of Jesse and anointed David he just did not jump up and walk into the fullness of his calling it took him years in order to become in the fullness of God, he took one step at a time. David is in the shadow of the order of Melchizedek as King-priest after the third anointing.

Psalms 92:10-11
Zion: The City of David; The holy Hill, A dwelling place, Mountain of Zion, Zion is Joyful, Zion travails Isaiah 66:8-blow the trumpet in Zion, Joel 2:1

We must learn to praise him through our trial, for we are partakers of Christ's sufferings. His glory will be revealed in us not to us. We are joyful even in our worst times of our lives. We are to stay joyful in the Lord. If the devil can steal our joy he can take our goods. Jesus said rejoice and be glad. The Lord made mornings for us, joy comes in the morning not at night. We do not have to battle the devil all day long then in the evening get victory. JOY COMES IN THE MORNING!

Ask boldly:

Hebrews 4:16
Let us therefore come boldly unto the throne of Grace, that we may obtain mercy, and find grace to help in time of need.

Christ sympathizes with our frailties, our shortcomings. It is call The Throne of Grace because it flows from love, it gives us help, mercy, and forgiveness. For Christ becomes our Great High Priest opening a way for us to obtain salvation and bring us back into God. Proverbs 28:1: Also the righteous are as bold as a lion. We must be bold, nowhere in the bible are we to be weak, we are to be bold as a lion. Acts 2:1-8; and when they prayed the place was shaken where thy all assembled together: They were FILLED with the Holy Ghost, and they spoke the Word of God with boldness. We have the inner power when we have the Holy Ghost within us. It gives us a motivation to go forth in the power and demonstration of the Holy Ghost. It gives us strength and power to slay our giants in our walk with the Lord. Remember boldness is going forth in the name of Jesus, weakness is going nowhere fast.

Ephesians 6:18
Praying ALWAYS with all prayer and supplications in the spirit, and watching thereunto with all perseverance and supplication for all saints.

Philippians 4:6
Be careful (anxious) for nothing; but in everything by prayer and supplication with thanksgiving let your request be known unto God.

How we must overcome our anxious thoughts:

1. Pray with all supplications; to make our petition known. To persevere, to be patient. We are to pray continually, meditate on the word. In other words have a continual prayer upon our lips.
2. Rejoice Matthew 5:12 Rejoice, and be exceeding glad; for great is your reward. We are to rejoice in the Lord! Our **Delight** is in the Lord (Greek) to be glad to be delighted, God speed
3. Thanksgiving:
   Jonah 2:9 But I will sacrifice unto thee with the voice of thanksgiving; I will pay that which I vowed. Salvation is of the Lord.
   Colossians 4:2 Continue in prayer, and watch in the same with thanksgiving. We are to lift up our voices in thanksgiving to give our sacrifice unto the Lord

Supplication (Greek) petition.
Perseverance (Greek) patience.

We are to always pray, to make our petition known unto God, we are to have patience, which is perseverance. We are not to be anxious we are to prevail.

Genesis 32:24-30
Jacob was left alone, and there he wrestled a MAN with him until the breaking of the day (dawn).
26th And he said let me go for the day breaks. And he said, I will not let you go, except thou bless me.
30th And Jacob said I will name this place Peniel: for I have seen GOD FACE TO FACE and my life is preserved.

I know what you must be thinking here! The bible says no man has seen God and lived. Let us go to the book of I John 4:12 No man has seen God at any-time, and St. John 1:18 says the same thing. Then in Genesis here is saying Jacob saw God face to face, and his life was preserved. Jacob wrestled all night and saw God face to face. Jacob told him, "I will not let you go till you tell me who you are", in other words reveal yourself to me. There is a type of death took place here, Jacob's name was changed here from Jacob to Israel. His hip was out of joint; a new walk. So Jacob's spirit man saw God face to face. The old Adam-nature died. Jacob's name in (Hebrew) means; heel catcher, replacer, a follower. Israel means; he struggles with God. Jacob came to the end of himself; he paid the price of deception, for he was deceived also. We must come to the end of our self in order for the Lord to reveal himself to us. We must wrestle with God all night, when we do we will be caught up in the spiritual realm for the Son to shine through our darkness and to praise him till the blessings flow; till it is no longer I! But only the Great I AM! That our lives to be caught up to meet him, He says in Revelation to come up hither. Come up hither, we do not have to die in order to obtain or achieve this encounter. This is one of the deceptions of the enemy. Same as Peter: Matthew 14:24-31; When he walked on the water, he saw God, he saw no flesh, he looked like a ghost to Peter. It scared him at first; but then Peter got out of the boat looking straight to Jesus. He did not realize he was raised up in the spirit, walking on top of the water, he defied all odds, Peter witnessed the Glory Of God here. Then Peter realized he was walking on top of the water and flesh took over and he began to sink. When we get caught up in the spirit at times we lose sight of our surroundings and we see nothing, feel nothing or have a care in this world. We are lost in the presence of the sweet Holy Ghost. This is called the glory realm, beyond worship where the Shekinah Glory is, what is called the glory cloud, the light of the

Holy Ghost. This is where we become one with God Almighty. We must persevere in order to enter in there-of. Apostle Paul said; this is pressing way in Philippians 3:14; I press toward the mark for the prize of the high calling of God in Christ Jesus. We must press through the crowd like the woman who had an issue of blood, she pressed through the crowd. She was under the old law, she had to have been a Jew to know where to touch his garment, if she was caught before she touched his hem (tassel) she would have been stoned, for she was unclean. She was to be kept away from people. The woman had to be crawling or bent down on her knees to touch the long corner tassel that was wrapped in very expensive blue thread. This is why Jesus knew he was touched for the virtue went out of him, she touched the secret place, got under the wing of the Almighty. She had faith to know if she touched the tassel of his garment she would be made whole. We must press through the crowd; we must get down on our knees or bow down to enter into the secret place as Psalms 91 says; He that dwells in the secret place of the Most High Shall abide under the shadow of the All Mighty. 4th He shall cover thee with his feathers, and under his wings shalt thou trust. We are to abide under the shadow (shade, protection) under his wing (corner, hem, borders, in a corner) and we are to be made whole, no longer in sin sickness, we will live and not die. For flesh cannot inherit the Kingdom of God, for flesh stinks in the knowledge of God. We must press through to persevere to the end.

We must have faith:

Hebrews 11:1
Now Faith is the substance of things hoped for, the evidence of things not seen.

Romans 14:17
So then faith comes by hearing (incline) and hearing by the word of God.

Romans 1:17
As it is written, the just shall live by faith.

Hebrews 11:6
For without faith it is impossible to please him; for he that comes to God must believe that he is, and that he is a rewarder of them that diligently seek him.

We see here we must declare by faith we are saved by and through his precious blood. We hear the word, we stand on the word by faith. We have a hope, an assurance that we have a heavenly Father, who sets on the throne. We have faith without wavering or doubting, we are to believe and have faith, not wavering that God sent his only Son to shed his precious blood for our sins. For without faith we cannot please God.

We Must Obey Wisdom:

We must obey **Wisdom** or our life is cut off from God spiritually speaking. Walk in the way of the Lord. **Wisdom** gives us a security, it keeps us walking steadfast in God.

Romans 12:2
And be not conformed to this world: but ye transformed by the renewing of your mind, that ye may prove what is good, and acceptable, and perfect will of God. **Conformed** (Greek) mold, fashioning, to pattern.

We are not let the circumstances of life to mold us or to let man mold us. We are not to pattern after someone else. We have certain people in our lives that leaves a good impression on us but we are in no means to pattern after them. I was a Praise and Worship Leader in the church where I was going, the pastor's wife played the piano and she sang, she is a great anointed singer, I always loved to hear her sing. I always said; "If I could sing like Sister Cathy I would be so happy." We had a weekend revival at church and after church I walked up to Sister Cathy she was talking to the evangelist and his wife, they were complementing me on my singing, Sister Cathy looked at them, then to me and said: "If I could only sing like Sister Sandy I be so happy." I was so shocked! But I learned a great lesson that night, we are never happy for what God has given us, we want what someone else has. God has given us a special anointing and special gifts they are just special made for us, use them to the fullness and know you are blessed from God with what you have. The **Wisdom** here is to know what God have given you, with **Wisdom** walk in the gifts, callings, election, whether they seem small or great, everything is important in the Kingdom of God or he would not have trusted you with what he gave you. We have no excuse to be ignorant of God's Word for it is written for our benefit to learn and grow by. We need **Wisdom** we must obey **Wisdom** we must continually seek **Wisdom.**

Notes

Chapter 8

How to Discern the Wisdom of God

How the natural Wisdom verses the Godly Wisdom

The Natural Wisdom:

1. **Worldly Wisdom**:

    Colossians 2:23
    Which things have indeed a shew of **Wisdom** in will worship, and humility, and neglecting of the body; not in any honor to the satisfying of the flesh.

    We are never to entertain flesh, flesh brings the opposite of humility it brings pride, the lusts of the flesh the lusts of the eyes, if it feels good, it looks good, but don't necessarily mean it is of God. It is devilish, pride is of the devil nothing good will come of it.

    James 3: 14-15
    But if ye have bitter envying and strife in your hearts, glory not, and lie not against the truth.
    15th This **Wisdom** descends not from above, but it is earthly, sensual, devilish.

16th For where envy and strife is; there is confusion and every evil work.

Envy (Greek) jealousy,

Envy is related to strife. It refers to selfish ambitions that prompt our own will or interests. Selfish ambitions in in the church world, refers to our own ways and it is earthly, it is sensual, in other words it is without the guidance of the Holy Ghost.

Selfish ambitions yielding to our selfish flesh verses the wiliness to yield to the Holy Ghost. A man is to show humility one to another, to be gentle yet strong, we are to speak words of **Wisdom** and know when to speak also. We cannot have bitterness in our hearts to one another, nor can we have strife among the brethren. God cannot get any glory out of us when we are chained to worldly things. We cannot lie against one another or lie against the truth, we cannot have envy or jealousy in our heart. Jealousy destroys everything in its path, it has destroyed homes, churches and families, jealousy is also a form of fear, and insecurity it is a spirit of defeat.

As we have read earlier the **Wisdom** is skillful she is wise, she built her house on seven pillars. Foolish woman is the total opposite.

Proverbs 9:13
A foolish woman is clamorous: she is simple (not disciplined, deceptive.) and knows nothing.
18th But he knows not that the dead are there; and that her guests are in the depths of hell.

A foolish woman knows nothing of preparing for her household. She thinks of herself and nobody else, if she thinks of someone else it has to do with how it has to better herself and nothing more. She eats the bread of idleness, a wise woman prepares her family for winter and a wise woman builds up, a foolish plucks up. A wise woman opens her mouth in **Wisdom**, a foolish woman opens her mouth with destruction.

II Corinthians 1:12
For our rejoicing in this, the testimony of our conscience, that in simplicity and godly sincerity, not with fleshly **Wisdom**, but by the grace of God, we have our conversation in the world, and more abundantly to you-ward.

We see here there is a natural or worldly **wisdom** the world knows and wants. This **wisdom** is satisfying the flesh such as; glory to self- will, bitterness, flesh, unspiritual, and natural. The natural **wisdom** is showing the world what we have, projecting flesh, verses Godly **Wisdom** which is projecting God The Father, it is not placing the spot light on our-self it is putting the spot light on God. It is all about God, not about ourselves. This natural worldly **wisdom** is not of God it is devilish this is satisfying the fleshly desires, This **wisdom** is not from above this is **wisdom** of self, putting honor to our flesh.

I Chronicles 15:29
And it came to pass, as the ark of the covenant of the Lord came to the city of David, that Michal, the daughter of Saul looking out at a window saw King David dancing and playing; and she despised him in her heart.

II Samuel 6:14-23
And David danced before the Lord with all his might; and David was girded with a linen ephod.
16th And as the ark of the Lord came into the city of David, Michal Saul's daughter looked through a window, and saw King David leaping and dancing before the Lord; she despised him in her heart.
Ephod (Hebrew) a garment of a priest used for adornment as an aid in priestly service. A skillful, woven covering.

21st And David said unto Michal, It was before the Lord, which chose me before thy father; and before all his house, to appoint me ruler over the people of the Lord, over Israel; therefore will I play before the Lord.
23rd Therefore Michal the daughter of Saul had no child unto the day of her death.

We see here very plainly the **wisdom** that Michal David's wife used that day as she looked out the wrong side of the window. Michal did not see the whole picture, she only saw in parts. She did not come out through the door of the house, if she did she would not have judged the matter incorrectly. If she even had went to the other window to see the full view she would not have judged the matter hastily. Michal judged her husband hastily for she was humiliated for he husband danced until his clothes fell off and revealed his undergarments. This is all she saw, she did not see the Ark was brought back to them was the reason David her husband was rejoicing, cause the ark was back in the midst of the people once more. We must be careful to use **Wisdom** in all things When Michal David's wife judged looking out of the wrong side of the window not seeing a full picture she cursed herself, she became barren not having a child. This does not mean being only barren in the natural, it can also mean barren in the spirit, to be cute off we must see the whole picture to reason the situation out before we pronounce judgment upon the matter.

The Godly Wisdom:

1. The Secrets of **Wisdom**

   Job 11:6
   And that he would shew the ***SECRETS*** of **Wisdom**, that they are double to that which is! Know
   Therefore that God exacteth of thee less than thine iniquity deserves.
   Secrets (Hebrew) hidden, things that are hidden.
   Exacteth (Hebrew) To make one forget, forgotten.

   Wisdom gives strength

   Eccl 7:19; 9:18
   Wisdom strengthens the wise more than ten mighty men which are in the city.
   18th **Wisdom** is better than weapons of war; but one sinner destroys much good.

   We recognize here the more of the **Wisdom** of God we have the stronger we become.

   Wisdom is skillful

   Daniel 1:4-17;
   Children in whom was no blemish, but well favored, and ***skillful*** in ***ALL Wisdom,*** cunning in

Knowledge, and Understanding science, and such as had ability in them to stand in the king's
Palace, and whom they might teach the learning and the tongue of the Chaldeans

Wisdom is pure

James 3:17
But **Wisdom** is first pure, then peaceable, gentle, and easy to be intreated, full of mercy and good fruits.

With **Wisdom** being pure, **Wisdom** brings peace that passes all understanding, gives peace within our spirit and soul. **Wisdom** is gentle, she is not hostile, or harsh, she speaks in love and harmony, giving fruit in due season.

Wisdom is meek

James 3:13
Who is a wise man and endued with Knowledge among you? Let him shew out of a good conversation his works with meekness of **Wisdom**.
Meekness: Greek Humbleness, humility, gentleness
Endued (Greek) clothed, putting on, arrayed

Wisdom is clothed in humility, she is gentle, she is humble, she wise in all her conversation. **Wisdom** is arrayed in Knowledge, she knows when to speak, when to keep silent, **She** knows when to stand still, and when to rise. **Wisdom** is not only gentle, humble and wise, she is pure.

The manifold **Wisdom**:
The manifold **Wisdom** of God has very many sides, as we have already encountered here in this brief study. ***Wisdom*** is first pure, meek, and strong, there are many facets of ***Wisdom***

Ephesians 3:10
To the intent that now unto the principalities and powers in heavenly places might be known by the church the manifold ***Wisdom*** of God.

There is a wellspring of **Wisdom**:

Proverbs 18:4
The words of a man's mouth are as deep waters, and the wellspring of **Wisdom** as a flowing brook.

In deep water you can very well drown if you are not careful, a mouthful of words out of a man's mouth without **Wisdom** is as deep and strong as deep waters. It will draw you asunder; but words of **Wisdom** flowing out of a wise mouth, is as refreshing as the water flowing in a waterfall. We are seeing here throughout the Bible we must have **Wisdom**, We must see the need for discernment (perceive, knowing) that goes hand in hand with **Wisdom**, Knowledge and Understanding. Discernment is also discerning; which is; distinguishing, passing. Discernment is seeing in the spirit what is going on in the church world. God reveals what is false, what is not of him. Discernment is knowing the right song to sing, the right message to preach, to know when to speak, when to be still. The Christian people has lost their vision, they have lost their way. They do not know how to study, to run reference to rightly divide the word of God. The pastor is not teaching his flock how to study, to know the full salvation plan, to know how the church is to be set in order. The Christians are not being taught how to stand in the evil days, for they are being preached the feel good, ear tickling doctrine. The Christians will not and do not how to stand in God's provision, to know who God really is. He is our refuge he is our shelter we are coming into the times we better know who Jesus is. How to enter into his rest, to hide in him to shelter us, there is a storm coming and our nature is too escape, to be in a comfort zone. We better be prayed up know the Word for that is our only refuge is in Jesus.

When we totally submit to the Holy Ghost we will resist the proud and become humble as a little child. We will not allow the lusts and envy come in our lives for we will not have room enough for it to enter we will be full of the Word. It is our daily prayer life, and studying to keep a holy life. God resists the proud and gives grace to the humble.

11 Chronicles 7:14
If my people which are called by my name, shall humble themselves and pray, and seek my face, and turn from their wicked ways; then will I hear from heaven, and will forgive their sin, and will heal their land.

Here he is talking to his people, not to sinners: For the people he said is the ones that are called by his name

There are five things we must do in order to get victory:

1. We must first hear.
2. We must humble ourselves
3. To pray

4. To seek his face
5. Turn from our from our wicked ways

Three Things God Will Do!

1. God will hear us
2. God will forgive us
3. God will heal our land, our earth, our bodies

I Corinthians 14:33
For God is not the author of confusion, put of peace, as in all churches of the saints.

We are to overthrow the words of a transgressors, not to allow confusion to enter in, we are to have peace, a gentle spirit, to season our words with grace. To speak with love and humility not with hostile word's or a hurtful spirit, they can wound a heart. When we speak the word, the Word will convict their heart and set them free from condemnation.

Isaiah 47:10
For thou hast trusted in thy wickedness: and thou hath said, none sees me. Thy **Wisdom** and thy knowledge, it hath perverted thee: and thou hath said in thine heart, I am, and none else beside me. There is only ONE I AM! Exodus 3:13-14; Moses asked God what do I say unto them? 14th I AM THAT I AM.

We are not to lean to our own understanding; nor can we look at what we have done, we have done nothing, The Lord works through us as his vessels, we cannot do anything less he works through us. Our flesh stinks in the nostrils of God; we are to look unto the Lord, where our help comes from. When we look at ourselves and say, "Look! What I have done! We are lifting up ourselves and God is not happy with that. We are not giving God the glory, we are glorying in our flesh. This is taking God's name in vain, we are using him for our vain glory. When we ask God to dam something, we are not taking his name in vain we are asking or telling God to dam whatever we are speaking or thinking of at the time we did it. Then we blame God for what happens in our lives. Taking God's name in vain is using God for our glory. When we are going through trials did we curse ourselves? Just remember not to lean to our own understanding. It is what the Lord has done, not what we have done.

We Are to Be Full of Wisdom And Holy Ghost:

Acts 6:3
Wherefore brethren look ye among you, seven men full of honest report, full of the Holy Ghost and **Wisdom**, whom ye may appoint over this business.

The Apostles stipulated that seven (mature, complete) men be full of the Holy Ghost, to have an honest report, in other words to have a good background in business, to have a good name, a reputation, to be a good steward of God's money. To have **Wisdom** to operate in the Holy Ghost. To express good character and quality within the believer. We are to be full of joy, to have the fullness of God, with an overflowing cup. Not to be full of strong drink but filled with the Holy Ghost.

Daniel 3:13-17
When King Neb-u-chad-nezzar was raged and in his fury commanded to bring Shadrach, Meshach, and Abed-ne-go, then they brought these men before the King.

14th Neb-u-chad-nezzar spoke unto them, is it true, O Shadrach, Meshach, Abed-ne-go, do you not serve my god's nor worship the golden image which I have set up?

16th Shadrach, Meshach and Abed-ne-go answered and said to the King, O Neb-u-chad-nezzar, we are not careful to answer thee in this matter.

17th If it be so, our God whom we serve is able to deliver us out of thine hand, O King.

Read all of chapter three here, in The Book of Daniel, for it too numerous to write it all down. I know we have heard this story of the three Hebrew boys of how God had delivered them from the furnace fire. We heard the logos word here many times over and it is good. There is a spiritual lesson that I am going to bring out here on how we must go through the furnace of affliction. God is delivering us through the fire not from the fire. Through the furnace fire we will suffer persecutions, will suffer rejections we will walk through the barren desert, the heat is so hot. Many times we have had to make some hard decisions in life weighing the matter heavily on our shoulders, not knowing which way to turn. Then a scripture come to mind through our much praying. We know we must stand on the Word, for that is what is going to take us through. We can take the easy way out but sometimes that is not the answer to the problem we are facing at this present time. For if we miss God there is too much of a heavy price to pay. I know you are probably wondering what has this to do with **Wisdom**, knowledge and Understanding. This has a lot to do with it. If the Hebrew boys looked at their own worldly **Wisdom**, knowledge and understanding they would have said this: "I do not want to die!" "The Lord will understand that I was forced to worship the idols". The golden image is just an image it is not real. I had

no choice in the matter. Then they would have not been thrown in the furnace fire, they would not have to face death, but when this **Wisdom** is used, it brings death not life spiritually. The Hebrew boys chose to not worship Idols they knew they were only one true God. They were thrown into the furnace, the furnace was raised up to be seven time hotter (perfection, maturity) they were bound with ropes, when they looked in the fire there were four men walking down there. The fourth man was like unto the Son of God. Daniel 3:25; They did not even smell like smoke they were no longer bound up they came out of the fires and lived. In our Christian walk with Lord, we have come to the crossroads of life, as the old saying between a rock and a hard place. When we are thrown into the furnace fires we have Jesus Christ within us to bring us through to burn off all the dross, to burn off traditions of men. Sometimes we must walk away from the comfort zone and walk a long hard road alone, like the Hebrew boys. The Lord says; woe to them that are in ease in Zion. But look at the victory here that is won here. The tables turned here. The King was who was real and who was an Idol. He promoted the Hebrew boys and the King worshiped their one true God. There is no stopping place. Paul said this is a race to the finish line.
Zion is (Hebrew) word. **Sion** is (Greek) word.

Hebrews 12:1-2
Wherefore, seeing we also are compassed about with so great CLOUD of Witnesses (People) (clouds do not speak), let us lay aside every weight, and the sin which does so easily beset us, and let us run with patience the race that is set before us.
2nd Looking unto Jesus the Author and Finisher of our faith. Who for the joy that was set before him endured the cross, despising

the shame, and is set down at the right hand (Power) of the throne in God.

I Corinthians 9:24
Know ye not that they which run in a race run all, but one receives the prize? So run, that ye may obtain.

Notes

Chapter 9

Receiving Wisdom In Your Life

II Corinthians 10:4-5
(For our weapons of our warfare are not carnal, but mighty through God to pulling down of strongholds).
5th Casting down imaginations; and every high thing that exalts itself against God, and bringing into captivity every thought to the obedience of Christ.
Imaginations (Greek) thought, argument, reasoning. Doubt

We see here according to the scriptures our warfare is in our minds, the battlefield of our own mind, we must fight flesh over spirit. The enemy first has to give us a thought in our minds. Then secondly we must ponder on the thought, thirdly we must to put it to action. We just do not go and sin out of nowhere. What we must do is when the enemy puts a thought in our mind is to have **Wisdom** to know it is not of God. We must rebuke the thought right away, not to think on it, or to dwell on the matter. When we rebuke the enemy we are resisting the enemy and the enemy has to flee. There is one more thing I want to stress here, there is only one Devil! He is not everywhere, he is not omnipresent like our Lord is. There is only One Omnipresent; that is God, he is everywhere. He can speak to all his people at the same time everywhere, the enemy cannot. The Devil has his demons (Demons is not in the bible but means the same) to do his work and deceit. When we say the Devil has been on our shoulder we are saying the devil is omnipresent, he is not, only God. He has his demons to war with us. We cannot look in the natural realm, we must look in the spiritual realm. We are to have discernment in order to look into the spirit to discern what is good and what is false, is it the enemy or is it God? Know the word, the more you know the word the more weapons you have against the Devil. Is it God buffing us or is it the Devil tormenting us? Let me give you an example on how much credit we give the devil. When you go on a trip you check your oil, fill us your gas tank if not you will run out of gas, it makes you late for church or an important engagement of some sort; what will be the first thing we do? We blame the devil. Well I do not believe it is the devil, or God either, it is negligence on your part it is your FAULT! We must weigh the matter carefully there are three persons we can fault, Self, devil, or God.

Four Steps to Bring Our thought Under the Lordship of Christ:

1. Beware that God knows every thought you think and there is nothing hid. Psalms 94:11;
2. Beware that the mind is the battlefield, resist the devil and he will flee from you. James 4:7.
3. Stay focused on Christ and heavenly things, rather than the earthly things. Fill your mind with God's word, it is life and peace and joy in the Holy Ghost. Colossians 3:2
4. Be careful of what you see, hear, smell, speak or touch (five senses). Do not let your eyes lust (lust of the eyes) after fleshly desires that are not of God. Nor listen to gossip, letting your ears be garbage cans. Lust of the flesh touching Genesis 3:3; 1 John 2:16; nor are we to gossip about one another.

Here are Steps to Aid in Our Salvation:

1. **Admit you do not know.**

   It is better to be honest than to fumble through and make a blunder of ourselves.

2. **Choose to pray before you speak.**

   We should be encouraged to intercede for our fellow Christian in need before we speak, for we may say something that can offend or cause our brother or sister to fall. Then we are in danger of having their blood required at our hands. Paul said;

   II Corinthians 1:11
   Ye also helping together by prayer for us, that the gift bestowed upon us by means of many persons thanks may be given by many on our behalf.

   James 3:13
   Who is a wise man and endued with knowledge among you? Let him show out of good conversation his works, with meekness of **Wisdom**.

   James 1:19
   Wherefore, my beloved brethren, let every man be swift to hear, slow to speak, slow to wrath.

   So we must choose our words wisely with **Wisdom,** and to have a wholesome mouth, a bridled tongue is a wholesome mouth. To be careful not to sow discord among the brethren, for we will stand for every idol word spoken.

3. **Wait Upon the Lord:**

Isaiah 40:31
They that wait upon the Lord shall renew their strength: they shall mount up with wings as eagles, they shall not run and not be weary; and they shall walk and not faint.
Wait (Hebrew) look for, gathered, to hope for, tarried.

Waiting on the Lord proves he will renew our strength, wait does not mean to do nothing; we are to tarry, (**persevere**) hope, to look for. We will mount up as an eagle in strength to soar above all birds, for the eagle is the king of all birds. The eagle flies above the clouds above all the oppositions, this refers to us having strength in the Lord to fly above all principalities of the air. We can soar in the strength of the Lord. We have a promise to arise above our needs and above our weaknesses, sufferings and trials. We can come out of our trials like an eagle soars to the sky. We have ability to run this race with patience and endurance. To walk without fainting.

4. **Rejoice:**

I Peter 4:12
Beloved think it not strange concerning the fiery trial which is to try you, as though some strange thing happen to you.
13th But rejoice, inasmuch as ye are partakers of Christ's sufferings; that then his glory shall be revealed, ye may be glad also with exceeding joy.

We must praise the Lord when we are going through a trial or a valley, this is the only way we can come out rejoicing and be victorious. When I was going through the worst time of my life I realized I had to look and see someone else in a worse condition then I was in, to pray for that person and rejoice through my sorrow. Not rejoice that I going through it rejoice for the Lord is bringing me out of it. The praise will not only bring you out of the situation but bring you through victorious to glean a nugget through your circumstance of life. When we see someone hurting worse it brings compassion to get our focus off ourselves. We do not need to set in our own misery all it brings is feeling sorry for ourselves, we need victory. We must not have envy and strife in our heart for it brings confusion to the body of Christ. God is not the author of confusion, for confusion is evil and it is devilish not Godly. We are to keep focus on our Lord and Savor; to seek his way not our way. **Wisdom** is; first pure then it brings peace to our hearts, it is gentle not hostile it brings us to be merciful and it causes us to produce good fruit.

Self- pity is not what we need, it is strength in the time of trouble or in the time of storm. It is the power of God we need! We must learn to praise the Lord or we cannot be victorious. What did the disciples do when they were in the boat when the storm hit? They panicked, they cried "we are going to Die!" they did not act on faith, they acted on fear. Fear is the opposite of faith, faith is the opposite fear. The disciples could have calmed the storm by speaking the power of the Lord. What I am saying here; if we have self- pity or we panic in our storms of life or wine around we will die. We are to stand up speak to our situation of life in our God given power and authority in Jesus name, with praise upon our lips Mark 4:36-41.

Remember no weapon formed against us shall prosper. When the storms of life hit, Be Still, watch and wait, listen, to get in the word and pray. The Lord will show us what to do. If we panic we do not use any good sense God has given us. We will run to and fro with every wind and doctrine confusing our minds not having a right mind set. We are not to allow confusion to enter our lives. God is not the author of confusion. This is where **Wisdom** come in at, **Wisdom** will show us when to move, where to go, when to speak. When we are in the storms of life come and our boat is rocking to and fro we can choose to fear and die, or we can choose faith to calm our storms of life; by speaking to the situations of life the Word and live. Remember, I said we learn by the things we suffer in life. We learn through every trial, every temptation, through every valley we walk and every mountain we climb. As a child learns through chastisement, correction, as he get older the correction get harder and harsher. They one day will grow up and be adult and thank you later that you loved them enough to correct them to get them ready for the world as an adult. This is the same way with our Heavenly Father, he loves those he chastises or corrects. As we start kindergarten we are learning the very basics of life, it gets rough on a small child to learn their numbers and their alpha-bet. Every grade level gets harder and more difficult, it takes discipline. Then we come to the last grade we are now a senior we have accomplished all we needed to get us to the next level, College. This took thirteen years of hard work to get us to this level, now we are ready for college. One semester is equivalent to one year of school it is on a faster scale. Our teachers we had in school are now Professors in college. We are not children no more we are adults in college. This is the same with our walk with the Lord, each step gets harder.

Hebrews 6:1
Therefore, leaving the principles of the doctrine of Christ, let us go on unto perfection; (maturity) not laying again the foundation of repentance from dead works, and of faith toward God.

In other words mature, grow up go on into more mature faith. You cannot stay on the milk. It is for babies and toddlers. We must grow up and eat the meat of the word.

1 Peter 2:2
As the babes, desire the sincere milk of the word, that ye may grow thereby.

Romans 8:14
For as many are led by the spirit of God, they are the **SONS OF GOD!**

Galatians 4:7
Wherefore thou art no more a servant, but a Son; and if a Son, then an heir of God through Christ.

We are to incline our ears to the spirit of God, we are to study to prepare ourselves for the next level in life. For each level gives us more **Wisdom**, knowledge and understanding in the Lord. The last trial I was in, I said "ok Lord you said to me I had to learn to praise you more." That you inhabit the praise of your people. It is very hard to praise the Lord when everything in your life has hit you full force all at once. All you want to do is cry, you are in shock, you are hurting, then comes the anger, you do not know which way to turn, your world collapsed it came to an end as you know it. You are in a state of master confusion you wonder what you did that was so wrong. You wonder if you can ever make it to the next breath the next second, never the less the next minute. All you want to do is die, to escape your hurt, your misery. Can you imagine ole Job what he suffered? Job did not curse God, he did not blame God, but in his devastation he did not lose faith nor did he lose hope. I felt in my despair I missed God, my life was over, but I sought God every morning, studied his Word, prayed, I never hardly left my home in three years. God revealed to me his Love how he loves each one of his children. He looks upon us with great compassion as a Daddy loves his Children. I praised him through this last trial, I am not saying they will not be any more trials, each trial gets harder till we come into perfection and we are complete in him. The Lord uses people to come your way to give you a word in due season, to give you a message in song. He will give you a vision, or a dream. He will speak to you in various ways. This is where **Wisdom** comes into play, to know you heard from God Almighty.

Let us go to Hannah:
I Samuel 1:17
2nd And he had two wives; the name of the one was Hannah, and the name of the other Peninah had children, but Hannah had no children.

9th So Hannah rose up after they had eaten in Shiloh, and after they had drunk. Now Eli the priest sat upon the seat by a post of the temple of the Lord,
10th and she was in bitterness of soul, and prayed unto the Lord, and wept sore.
11th And she vowed a vow, and said, O Lord of Hosts, if thou wilt indeed look on the affliction of thine handmaid and remember me, and forget thine handmaid, but wilt give unto thine handmaid a man child, Then I will give him unto the Lord all the days of his life, and there shall be no razor come upon his head.
13th Now Hannah she spake in her heart; only her lips moved, but her voice was not heard: therefore Eli thought she had been drunken.
14th And Eli said unto her, How long wilt thou be drunken? Put away thy wine from thee.
15th And Hannah answered and said, No, my Lord, I am a woman of a sorrowful spirit; I have drunk neither wine nor strong drink, but have poured out my soul before the Lord.
17th Then Eli answered and said, Go in peace; And the God of Israel grant thy petition that thou hast asked of him.
We see a picture of Hannah in her despair, she sees Peninah her husband's other wife she has children. In the Old Testament if you did not have a son you were despised, treated with contempt; afflicted among your own people. Hannah; as we see here went to the house of the Lord, she fasted and wept. She cried so hard and caught up in the spirit here; she moved her lips but no words were spoken out of her mouth, Eli the priest thought she was drunk. There is a great lesson here on how Eli saw Hannah, he looked and saw her and he

condemned her. He did not use any **Wisdom**, nor did he see nothing in the spirit he was in the flesh too busy to condemn. This is so much like the Christian people are today. There is a saying that pans out to be much truth in it. Believe nothing you hear, and half what you see, for what you see can be totally different, then you judge the matter in total ignorance.

Matthew 7:1-2
Judge not, that ye be judged.
2nd For with what judgment ye judge, ye shall be judged; with what measure ye mete, it shall be measured to you again.
Mete (Greek) measure,
Measure (Greek) limit, what is apportioned

Eli did not know the difference in a sorrowful spirit then a drunken spirit, this is sad. But through him being busy judging Hannah; Hannah's prayer was answered. Hannah's husband spoke to his wife he told her to go in peace her petition was granted, he spoke with faith and stood on faith.

5. Ask Boldly:

Hebrew 4:16
Let us come Boldly unto the Throne of Grace, that we may obtain Mercy, and find Grace to help in the time of need.
Grace (Hebrew) favor, well favored, gracious, (Greek) kindness, blessing, gift, benefit, acceptable.

Jesus Christ sympathizes with our weaknesses and our short comings! It is called The Throne of Grace for a reason. Grace flows from above. Grace gives us favor with the Lord Grace gives us benefits, gives us kindness, Grace accepts us where we are at. For ***Jesus Christ*** is our ***GREAT HIGH PRIEST!*** Opening up a way for us to obtain salvation and bring mankind back to himself. When Jesus was conceived he took upon himself the likeness of sinful flesh.

Romans 8:3-4
For what the law could not do, in that it was weak through the flesh, God sending his own Son in the likeness of sinful flesh, and for sin, condemned sin in the flesh.
4th That the righteousness of the law might be fulfilled in us, who walk not after flesh, but after spirit.

Might is a poor translation everywhere it is written in the bible it is doubtful, maybe could be, or a possibility. Where <u>might</u> is used should be replaced with <u>will</u>.

I believe I got this part from Bob Torango. "Jesus partook of the Mitochondrial D.N.A. of Mary to obtain the direct line back into the genetic logos of Adman's fall. He not only dealt with sin in the spirit, he dealt with it in the flesh!" We bear both genetics or like any other creature made. We are a redeemed man. We bear both genetics, Father's D.N.A. and pre-fallen D.N.A."

When Jesus went to the cross he was the second Adam or the Last Adam. When God took the rib (side, door) of Adam there was a type of death burial and resurrection took place here. When the bible talks of sleep it talks of death. The God brought forth Eve out of the side of Adam. When Eve partook of the tree of good and evil she was deceived. Adam took of the fruit with his eyes opened, he knew if did not take the fruit with her she would forever be lost. Adam chose to save Eve, he loved her enough to die for her and die with her. Adam died by the tree. Jesus went to the cross died on the tree. When Jesus gave up the Ghost and died, they pierced his side, water and blood flowed and Eve the church was born or birthed. This is a great illustration between Jesus and the church; and the greatest love story to mankind.

We are living in the seventh day from Adam and the third Day of Jesus Christ, or the third feast; The Tabernacle representing 100 trillion booths called cells containing a complete entire blueprint of the entire organism which is the human body.

Colossians 1:16-17
For by him were all things created, that are in heaven, and that are in earth, visible and invisible, whether they be thrones, or dominions, or principalities, or powers; all things were created by him and for him.
17th And he is before all things, and by him all things consist.

Proverbs 28:1
The wicked flee, when no man pursues; but the righteous are bold as a lion.

Proverbs 30:30
A lion which is strongest among beasts, and turneth not away for any

A lion is in the cat family, they are strong and courageous, for they are bold and fierce.
There is nowhere in the lids of the Bible we are to be weak, or we will die.

Ephesians 6:10
FINALLY! My brethren, ***BE STRONG IN THE LORD!*** And in the ***POWER of his MIGHT!***

I feel Apostle Paul is saying; Finally you are getting there, getting strong in the Lord, what has taken you so long brethren.

6. ***Perseverance:***

Ephesians 6:18
Praying always, with all prayer and supplication in the Spirit, and watching thereunto with all ***perseverance*** and supplication for all saints
Supplication (Greek) request, petition.
Perseverance (Greek) patience.

Philippians 3:14
I press toward the mark for the prize of the high calling of God in Jesus Christ.
Mark (Greek) goal.
Prize (Greek) foot race.

We are in this race for our life. We must press through as the woman with the issue of blood, or we will die. We must endure with all longsuffering, to be patient, always with a prayer upon our lips, coming from within our heart, mind and soul.

7. **Declare by Faith:**

I have the **Wisdom** of God! I am not saying just have faith and your faith wavers like the sea in a storm. Wavering faith is one day you say you got it, next day saying; "Well I Don't Know!" I got healed yesterday but the pain is back worse today, I just do not think I got healed. When the pain leaves and you know by faith you are healed, the devil will try the next day to bring the pain back full force to make you believe you did not get healed. You praise the Lord, you stand on the Word, and whose report you going to believe. The next day you still are healed, you have to stand on faith. You cannot doubt if you do; it is okay to pray "Lord help my unbelief" go to the healing scripture pray those scriptures and declare and decree them, pray the Father in Jesus name. We all know the famous scriptures on faith; Faith cometh by hearing and hearing by the Word of God. Faith is the substance of things hoped for and the evidence of things not seen. If we see it then it is not faith. We must have a hope, we must have an assurance, that we must walk by faith not by sight, wavering or doubting. Our sight is flesh; and flesh cannot obtain the deep things of God.

8. **Obey Wisdom:**

We must obey **Wisdom** in our life, or we are cut off from God spiritual and natural. Walk in the way of the Lord. **Wisdom** gives us security; it keeps us walking safely in God.

Romans 12:2
And be not conformed (Patterned) to this world; but be ye transformed (changed) by the renewing of your mind

We are to never to pattern after any man, or to let man mold us, only God can mold you into him, not man. When we study the Word we are applying the word into our heart. We are to pattern ourselves after Jesus Christ, to put on Jesus Christ to set our affection on him not on man. We are to love and respect people lift them up, but never to look to them as lord or praise them. Everything we say and do it must line up with the word. If you say you heard from God, or you had a vision or dream if it does not line up with the Word of God then it did not come from God for God will not go against his Word. **Wisdom** is the most vital in our walk with the Lord, it brings knowledge it bring understanding. Get **Wisdom**, it is the principle thing.

Notes

Chapter 10

We are to Grow up in Faith

Ephesians 4:13-15
Till we ALL COME in the UNITY of the FAITH, and of the knowledge of the Son of God, unto a PERFECT man, unto a measure of the stature of the fullness of Christ.
15th But speaking the truth in love, may grow up in him in all things, which is the head, even Christ.

We are to grow up in faith in the knowledge of God. Without wavering or without doubting. To become the perfect man (mature) to grow up in the fullness of Christ speaking the truth, every man a liar and God the truth.

Galatians 3:11-12
But no man is justified by the law in the sight of God, it is evident: for, the just shall live by faith.
12th And the law is not faith; but, the man that does them shall live in them.

In other words; we cannot live under the law, and try to live under Grace, it is impossible. The law brings death, Grace bring life. There is no more condemnation in those who are in Christ Jesus.

Galatians 3:24-26
Wherefore the law was our schoolmaster to bring us unto Christ, that we might (**will**) be justified.
25th But after faith is come, we are no longer under a school-master. 26th For ye are all the children of God by faith in Jesus Christ.
School-master (Greek) supervisor, instructors, guardian, custodian.

In other words the Old Testament (Old Covenant) concealed the New Testament (New Covenant). We could not live under the law for it brought death not life. The Old Testament is full of prophesies of the coming of the coming Messiah to redeem us from the law of sin and death.
The Holy Ghost is now our Teacher to lead and guide us into all truth.

Galatians 4:4-5
But when the fullness of the time was come, God sent forth his son, made of a woman, made under the law.

The church had to have faith to establish the first church in Acts after the Day of Pentecost.

II Corinthians 5:7
For we walk by Faith not by sight.

Hebrews 11:1-40
This is traditionally called the Faith Chapter.

Like I said earlier if we see it then it is not faith. But if we see it done or completed in the spirit, then it comes to past like we vision it to be, then that is faith in action. We must know we have heard from God, whether it be by the Bible, in a vision, to have a dream, or the Lord has spoken in an audible voice, but always remember it will line up with the Word, in any way you believed you have heard from the Lord. As I have shown to you here in the pages of this book of the Patriarchs of Old, how they went by faith. Let us look at Abraham; God told him to heave his Father Terah's home, Abraham knew without a shadow of a doubt he heard from God to leave his Father's house. We see here he left his comfort zone in order to obey his heavenly Father. God told Abraham to go until he told his to stop. Now this is full blown faith, it is out there. When God tell us to go somewhere he usually tells us where to go, then we pray and seek God to get the time, and place or something, but to go till he tells you to stop. I believe he told him what direction but not the actual place he was to go. So we see here Abraham went I believe he heard what we call an Audible voice. By faith Abel gave a more excellent sacrifice, how is that? He gave a blood sacrifice. By faith Enoch was translated that he did not see death.

Translated (Greek) to change (from one place or position to another). To take away. Carried over or transferred.

By faith Noah being warned of God of things not seen. God told Noah to build an ark, for it was going to rain. Noah had never seen rain. The water came up from the ground and watered the earth. Can you imagine for one minute being in Noah shoes? Not only did he hear from God; but he began to preach to the people and did so for one hundred years to relay to them what God told him.

They probably said to each other:

"Did you hear what Noah said; in service this morning?"
"I think Noah has really lost his ever loving mind this time."
"Why is that?"
"Did you not hear what he came off with this time?"

"Yes, I think I heard him right; but I was afraid I heard him wrong."
"Oh no Brother, you heard him right!"
Noah said; "People; we must prepare ourselves for a flood is coming."
"For whatever that is, he said God told him to build an ark!"
"What?"
"Yes, can you believe all that now?"
"We do not even know what an ark is!"
"Well what is rain? I never heard of that either."
"He told us that God told him to build it out of gopher wood; and to make it three stories high. He has to gather all the animals, both male and female; and seven each of the good kind. And not only that; but he actually wants us to help him."
"Who does he think he is?"

Sound funny to you? Yes it does, but probably not far off what they were saying about Noah in that day. I thought I would add a little hummer.

By faith Sarah conceived in her old age. Can you imagine this? She had gone through the change of life, and no doubt was white headed. Probably, she was kind of bent over from old age and possibly no teeth. She may not be able to hear too well anymore; and cannot see very well either. She probably had aches and pains as well. It is not any wonder Sarah laughed. But, then God began to change her, she began to get some color to her hair till it turned back to the original color. Her teeth began to grow back. Sarah started to stand straight once more and her ears were opening up. Her eyesight was coming back; and the change of life was beginning to be reversed. Then Sarah conceived and bore a son. By faith Isaac blessed Jacob and Esau. By faith Joseph, when he died, made mention of the departing of the Children of Israel. By Faith Moses when he came to years (**in other words maturity**) refused to be called the son of Pharaoh's daughter. Moses refused to be no longer a slave to bondage by the Pharaoh. He knew he did not belong to the worldly **wisdom** of man's traditions, so he fled. By faith he kept the Passover, and the sprinkling of the blood. By faith the walls of Jericho fell down. By faith Rahab perished not with them that believed not. She believed the spies and she helped them, so not only was she saved, but all that were in her household as well that day.

Romans 11:33
Who through faith subdued kingdoms, wrought righteousness, obtained promises, stopped mouths of lions.
Subdued (Greek) conquer, defeat, overcome. **Wrought** (Greek) to work, accomplish, to be active, commit, labor, minister.

The patriarch of old through faith; they conquered and defeated kingdoms, they were overcomers through obedience to God. They worked, labored, and worked to accomplish all that God called them to do. We have read and studied the patriarchs of old, things did not come easy to them by no means. God shown the patriarchs of old and how to pave the way for him to come as the Messiah; to come as a babe in the manger, to come and die on the cross of Calvary for our sins, to raise on the third day to bring us life and life more abundantly.

James 2:17-18
Even so faith, if it had not works, is dead being alone.
18th Yea, a man may say. Thou hast faith and I have works; shew me faith, without thy works, and I will shew thee faith my faith by my works

Works (Greek) deeds, labor, task

As we draw a picture in our mind of the patriarchs of old, how they activated their faith, by manifesting their faith by working in faith. The patriarchs not only heard from God they activated their faith in labor, deeds and in tasks. When Abraham heard from God to leave his father's house, he could have set there and just talked about it and never made any effort to activate his faith. When Noah being warned of God could have frozen in fear, saying to God I cannot go tell anyone Lord! They think I lost my mind! And we all would have perished. There is Moses; I am slow of speech, I cannot go tell Pharaoh what you want me to tell him, but Moses went with his Brother Aaron with a staff in his hand to face Pharaoh to set his people free. Joshua and Caleb they went to spy out the land to conquer the giants, they could have just talked about going and never got there. See what I am saying? Talk is cheap that Is all it is, cheap. But when you put action to your talk and faith to back you up you can conquer everything God told you to do. True faith manifests itself through obedience toward God, to be compassionate as a believer building on your most holy faith. There is saving faith is always a living faith that does not stop with mere confession of Jesus Christ our Savor, but prompts obedience to him as Lord. Only to those who believe, and only those who can obey. True faith is not only knowing you heard from the Lord, true faith is enduring faith, which shape our very existence. We are to know that we maintain a living faith not solely on our own efforts, but by the Grace of God, the indwelling **Holy Ghost**.

Romans 1:17
For therein is the righteousness of God REVEALED from faith to faith: as it is Written: The just shall live by faith.

We must have faith from start to finish; we need to live by it also. We as righteous people of God must live by faith, to grow. Thereby, we grow up in our most holy faith.

Different Types of Faith

Common faith

Titus 1:4
To Titus mine own son after the common faith: Grace and mercy, and peace, from God the Father and the Lord Jesus Christ our Savior.
Common (Greek) unholy, impure, defiled (Ceremonially)

Titus was after the ungodly defiled impure faith, of his son, talking to him about The Grace of God, to have peace from God the Father.

Weak Faith:

Romans 4:19
And being not Weak in faith, he considered not his own body now dead, when he was an hundred years old, neither yet the deadness of Sarah's womb.

We have weak faith, the kind that constantly limits us, due to wrong teachings, people who constantly argues and condemns each other over small matters of our lives. This usually consists of what we wear, How we have our hair, what we say, what we drink, or eat.

Romans 14:17
The Kingdom of God is not meat and strong drink; but righteousness, peace and joy in the Holy Ghost.

Strong Faith:

Giving glory to God
Romans 4:21-22
Being fully persuaded that what He promised he was able also to perform.
22nd And therefore it was imputed to him for righteousness.
Imputed (Greek) To credit, regard, accounted, count.

The strong faith it speaks of here is to know and to be fully persuaded that whatever God had promised he will perform it. Regardless of the circumstances that comes our way or whatever the cost may be if God said it, stand on it, in the most holy faith.

Little Faith:

Matthew 6:30
"Wherefore, if God so clothe the grass of the field, which today is, and tomorrow is cast into the oven, shall he not much more clothe you, O ye of little faith."

St. John 20:29
Jesus said unto him, *"Thomas because thou hast seen me, thou hast believed, blessed are they that have not seen, yet have believed."*

Thomas did not have the faith to believe that the Lord Jesus had not arose unless he first seen. Being that he doubted and then saw that is not faith.

Great Faith:

Matthew 8:5-10
And when Jesus was entered into Capernaum, there came unto him a Centurion, beseeching him.
6th And saying, Lord my servant lies at home sick of the palsy, grievously tormented.
7th The Centurion answered and said, my Lord I am not worthy that thou should come under my roof: But speak the **Word Only, and my servant shall be healed!**
10th When Jesus heard it, he Marveled, and said unto them that followed, "*Verily,* (truly) *I say unto you, I have not found* **SO GREAT FAITH**. *No not in Israel.*"
Palsy: (Greek) lame, paralytic, paralyzed.
Centurion (Greek) An officer.
Beseeching (Greek) to plead, to comfort, invite, urge

Not only do we see this man having Great faith, we see a great love for his fellow servant. This man was nothing to him, not a relative, not a best friend, not even an in-law. This scripture said he was nothing more than a servant or a slave. We see his servant got sick and was in great pain. This man was not thinking of the money he was no doubt losing by this man not only being sick, he is getting worse, he could have let him go to get rid of him. The love and compassion he had for his servant he wanted him healed. No doubt he took him to doctors to no avail. He heard Jesus was in town, so the officer went to town looking for Jesus for he had such great faith to know if he found him his servant would be healed. The officer found him and he urged him to heal his servant, he told him I am not worthy for you to come to my house (heart) But you can come to my servant's house (heart) Jesus looked at him seen the love in his heart to his fellow servant; he seen the great and marvelous faith,

Jesus reached out and I believed not only healed his servant but blessed him as well. The Lord said he had not seen such great faith. This officer had more faith then his disciples had, and they walked with him, they ate with him, they witnessed miracles everywhere he walked, for three and half years.

Active Faith:

James 2:14
What doth it profit, my brethren, though a man say he hath faith, and have not works? Can faith save him?

Faith does not save us by any means, but it takes faith to believe when you confess with your mouth the Lord Jesus Christ and believe in your heart, that salvation is made by confessing by faith. Faith without works is dead. We see by studying the faith chapter it would not do any good to have faith if we do not put it to action. The old saying goes; Actions speaks louder than words! We can talk faith all day but we MUST ACTIVATE IT! We must go beyond the stage of just hearing, we must apply it in order for it to work effectively.

Romans 11:6
But without faith it is impossible to please him; for he that comes to God must believe that he is, and that he is a rewarder of them that diligently seek him.
We see here that when we come to God we must believe, we must have faith, and the Holy Ghost must first draw us, we must confess.

The Importance of Faith:

We must diligently (earnestly, carefully) seek the Lord. Wise men still seek him, the wise men travelled from afar to find the Christ child. How far will we go, and what gifts to we have to bring? We have our mind, our heart and our soul to bring to him and we bow humbly before Jesus Christ. We cannot come to Jesus half-heartedly. We must realize the importance of faith, no prayer can be effective without faith. There is no limit to what faith is, or no limit to where we can go in faith.

Matthew 21:21
Jesus answered and said unto them, Verily, (truly) I say unto you, if ye have faith and doubt not, ye shall not only do this which is done to the fig tree, but also if ye shall say unto this mountain, be thou removed, and cast into the sea; it shall be done.

This right here is talking about the mountains in our everyday lives. We have mountains to climb, or we can choose walk around the mountain, but then we keep going around the same mountain not going anywhere. We must climb the mountain in order to conquer the mountain in our lives. Mountains gives us strength to withstand the battles in life. We can ask God sometimes to move the mountain, but we should ask him to help us climb the mountain, when we climb the mountain and we got to the other side the mountain is removed out of our sight. The children of Israel they went around the same mountain for forty years, all they did was grumble and complain until they died, not receiving the promise land.

The General Facts Concerning Faith

Faith can grow unlimited:

II Corinthians 4:13
We having the same spirit of faith, according as it is written, I believed, and therefore have I spoken; We also believe, and therefore speak.

Galatians 5:6
For in Jesus Christ neither circumcision avails anything, nor uncircumcision; but faith which works by love.

Ephesians 6:16
Above all, taking the shield of faith, wherewith ye be able to quench all the fiery darts of the wicked.

With faith picking up the shield of faith, knowing it will stop the fiery darts of the enemy. What is a fiery dart? A dart set on fire. Or it could be to not even feel the fiery dart, to send it back to where it came from in the name of Jesus.

Hebrews 6:12
That ye be not slothful, but followers of them who through faith and patience inherit the promises.

To those who endure by faith not wavering shall receive the promise. We must be true and faithful enduring what comes our way through faith and being faithful to our Lord to the end.

The Word Faith is found only twice in the Old Testament. The word trust is just another word (in the Old Testament) for faith and belief. Now faith is the assurance of things hoped for. Faith is knowing that in the spirit, you are to go forth in knowing you are in the Lord.

Divine Faith:

Hebrews 11:3
Through faith we understand that the worlds were framed by the word of God, so that things which are seen were made of things which do appear.

Faith is not only works in the natural; but it is an attribute of God. God through faith framed the worlds by the spoken word. God spoke the world into existence.

Romans 14:23
And he that doubteth is dammed if he eat, because he eateth not of faith: for whatsoever is not of faith is sin.

Wow you cannot get any plainer than this, can you? We must see the importance of faith, for without faith we are like a sea with billowing waves, tossing to and fro. If we do not have faith it is a sin, we must grow in faith by using our faith.

James 1:6
But let him ask in faith, nothing wavering, for he that wavers is like a wave of the sea driven with the wind tossed.

Rich Faith:

James 2:5
Hearken, my beloved brethren, hath not God chosen the poor of this world rich in faith, and heirs of the kingdom which he hath promised to them that love him?

We being rich in faith, rich is spirit, he has promised through our faith that we are an heir to the Kingdom.

The Gift of Faith:

I Corinthians 12:9
To another faith, by the same spirit; to another the gifts of healing by the same spirit;

There is a gift of faith it is more than a measure, there are nine spiritual gifts that is poured out without measure, to use in the body of Christ. But it is all in one spirit.

What Faith is Not:

Faith is not! I say faith is not a Feeling!!!
Faith is not a Wish!
Faith is not a Name it and Claim it!
Faith is not a Santa Claus in the spirit!
Faith is not Slack!
Faith is not Lack!
Faith is no wavering!

Faith is not based on what we say, it is not based on our merits, or what status we may have in the church. Faith is based on the word of God. We cannot be like Thomas and have virtually no faith. Or like the disciples who had fear versus faith. When the storms of life come in like a flood, we cannot stand up and say, "Here we go, I knew it, we are going to die just like I thought." Or are we going to see before we believe then that is not faith. We are our own worst enemy. We bring a lot of things on our own self through doubt and unbelief.

Proverbs 18:21
Death and life are in the power of the tongue; and they that love it shall eat the fruit thereof.

So if we say we cannot make it, then so be it. If we say we can do it, then we can do all things through Christ who strengthens us. This is faith standing on God's word. Faith is not in action; if we get prayer for our healing, we say we felt the power of God the pain is gone, then by time we get home or get up in the morning the pain is back with a vengeance worse than ever before. We do not look in the natural and say we did not get healed you did get healed. The devil came in and set on your shoulder and told you I told you did not get healed, you made a fool out of yourself. What you do is to stand on the promises of God you look the devil in the eye you quote the word tell him to get behind you, bind him tell him that you are healed. Then you thank the Lord, you quote the word, you praise him till the pain is gone, then you will get the victory in Jesus name. We must stand and activate out most holy faith. We must have strong faith, not to wine around; speak the word, stand on the word activate the word. Faith is not, the slightest relationship with feelings and sense evidences. There has been men think they have strong faith, all the faith in the world, that is right, all the faith in the world (flesh). When it has been just on feelings, feelings will not stand in the most trying times, These men find out they had the least of faith. A good man must learn to fight a good fight of faith. Strong faith is when you get diagnosed with stage two breast cancer, the kind that's very invasive, the doctor wants to do surgery A.S.A.P set up with six different Doctors for you to see in a matter of ten days, then do the surgery. Then we start a prayer line for several states around. We stood on faith, quoted the word; prayed the word. Then activated the Word. The Lord spoke into my spirit you do not have time for the devil. Then he spoke to me again, He brought the Word to my heart; whose report are you going to believe? My mother met the woman within a few days after my diagnoses she spoke to her, prayed with her told her I was going to be fine. My mother never saw the woman before or after. Then life- long friend of the family told mom she isn't going to have surgery I see Sandy Healed. My fiancé' looked right into my eyes and told me you do not have time for fear, we must activate your faith now. I went to all the Doctors in the matter of two weeks, by the time I got to the last Doctor he said: he virtually could not find the lump that was very huge two weeks before. Many people prayed with me, stood by me, had faith with me, and I believed in their prayers, but I had to activate it and believe to receive. This was a storm in my life that hit me less than a year ago, if I had weak or wavering faith I would not be here writing this book. The just shall live by faith.

Faith is Not Wavering:

We must take the word of God, be strong in the power of his might, to act upon it. Faith is refusing doubt, unbelief, and wondering. We count it done regardless of the evidence that shows different. Faith is to stay active, to be strong in the power of his might. Keep up the faith, if we must; pray and ask God to help your unbelief, I have had to in several circumstances in my life. You know it is proven, it is easier to die than it is to live, so you must press through till you know you made a break through. Faith is a continual action. It keeps on going in every aspect of our lives.

Faith is Not Temporary:

That kind of faith is to believe for a season or for a while until things do not go according to what we think. When the trials and temptations come, we fall short of the glory of God. There is nowhere in the lids of that Bible that we are to stop at just mere faith, we must continue in our faith walk.

Acts 14:22
Confirming the souls of the disciples, and exhorting them to continue in the faith, we must through much tribulation enter into the kingdom of God.

Faith is Not Dead:

The true kind of faith is strong and great, unwavering faith. It is faith that brings results in our lives. It is the true faith that brings action through the word of God. It brings unfeigned faith which is no shame, for it is not counterfeit. This faith is true, it is genuine, it is not bragging on self, no outward show of flesh. It proceeds out of the heart. It is unselfish, honest and pure.

This is great **Wisdom** spoken here on faith. **Wisdom** is in every aspect of our lives.

Notes

Chapter 11

Is it Life or is it Death

Proverbs 18:21
Death and life are in the power of the tongue: And they that love it shall eat the fruit thereof.

Proverbs 12:18-19
There is that speak like the piercings of the sword: but the wholesome tongue of the **Wise** is health.
19th The lip of truth shall be established forever; but a lying tongue is but for a moment.

What is done to you is of little account, what is done IN YOU is what it is accounted for, and the latter may be good or bad. Our feelings may be cut to the quick, very cruel and like a knife cutting us (like a piercing sword) to the core of our very being.

Proverbs 18:14
The spirit of a man will sustain his infirmity; but a wounded spirit who can bear?

One of the commandments are: thou shalt not kill. This should have been translated; Thou shall not murder. There is a considerable difference in these words here; with Kill and murder. Let me explain these words here in more detailed description. If we say thou shalt not kill, how do we explain Ecclesiastes 3:3? There is a time to kill. Now if we take the Ten Commandments thou shalt not kill and Ecclesiastes 3:3; We should say the Bible is contradicting itself, this is not so. This is why it should have been translated thou shall not murder. Murder is taking someone's life, or destroying their influence or their spirit. Ones attitude to another may be deeply be affected by a mere whisper. We are same as a murderer if we wound someone with our tongue. We can destroy our brothers and sisters cut them to the core with our tongue, believe it or not beliefs and convictions are formed by words, and they either destroy a man or they are a making of a man. Which are we doing? Then we go to the word kill, you kill for meat to eat and clothing to wear. Then you go to David who killed a lion, he killed a bear, he did not murder them he killed them. Which are we doing murdering or killing? What is murder? When we murder we are taking someone's life. Cain murdered his brother Able, he took his brother's life in his own hands. We must understand and know how to balance out the word of God, to get a proper balance or it becomes uneven and the scales are off balance. The other part of murder is when we are not giving the body, soul, and spirit realm. We have in times past (still some today) preached in the body and soul realm that produces death unto the body of Christ. But when we preach all three realms we have preached the balance of the true word of God. Remember everything balances in threes. **Wisdom**, Knowledge Understanding; The blood, The Word, The Name; The Father, The Son, The Holy Ghost, (un-separable). **Wisdom** in our lives brings forth life in the Word of God.

Matthew 15:11
Not which goes into the mouth that defiles a man; but that which comes out of the mouth, this defiles a man.
Defiles (Greek) Pollutes, call common

Proverbs 18:19
A brother offended is harder to be won than a strong city; and their contentions are like the bars of a Castle.

Mark 7:18-20
And he said unto them, are ye without **Understanding** Also? Do you not perceive, that whatsoever thing from without enters into the man, it cannot defile him.
19th Because it enters not into his heart, but into his belly, and it goes out into the draught, purging all meats.

In other words we digests our food and drink and our bodies gleans all the nutrients from the foods and when our body is finished gleaning it empties (**purges**) what it does not need. And he said, that which comes out of the man that defiles man.

Purges (Greek) Cleanse, purify.

It is saying here it is not what we put in our bellies that defiles a man, it is what we hold in our hearts. We hold grudges, bitterness, hurt, hatred, a get even attitude (spirit), wounds that will not heal from our bad experiences that holds us hostage. When you begin to realize that person you have hated for years or you have a problem with, you are letting that person hold you hostage. You may as well hand him a pair of handcuffs and let him bind you to him while he goes on with his life not even giving you one thought, if he is, he is laughing at you, for you give him full reign or full control of your life. You have let him be lord of your life, lord of you heart, mind and soul. Let go of this matter by talking to God. To pray for the Lord to heal your wounded spirit, to help you to let go, there is nothing you can do for it has already been done and it cannot be reversed. This is why the Lord said we must forgive. When we have these things in our heart we speak from our hearts. We speak out negativity, anger, hatred, and envy, like I said earlier a wounded heart who can heal? It takes God! We must come to the end of ourselves. We ask God to show help us to learn from life's lesson, and go on and be set free, if not this bitterness will cause cancer, organ failure, blood pressure problems it is not worth the price.

Proverbs 12:18-19
There is that speaks like piercings of a sword: but the tongue of the **wise** is health.
19th The lips of truth shall be established forever; but a lying tongue is but for a moment.

When we are in the Lord and have the Holy Ghost to bridle our tongues, we allow the Holy Ghost to speak truth to us. When we do not give credence to the Holy Ghost, we allow our tongues to be loosed, like a piercing sword and to cause destruction to our lives as well as others lives.

Proverbs 11:1
A false balance is an abomination to the Lord; but a just weight is his delight.
Balance (Hebrews) A pair of scales, (two) pans for weight measurement, as emphasis on honesty.

A pair of scales with the shaft in the middle and a bowl on each side if you put one pond on the left side and two pounds on the right side you will not have a balance. The left be up real high while the right will be way low. Try putting one pound in each bowl you will have a correct balance with the shaft holding the bowls. As you see it is a representation of Christ being the center and we being the bowls, we are to have a balance or we are an abomination unto God. This is the way in the Lord, number three is the balance as you see here. All through the Bible we see that there is number three and anywhere there are three's there is life.

There are three levels of the ark.
There are the three Hebrew Boys thrown in the furnace fire.

Jonah in the belly of the whale; for three days and three nights:

Jonah 2:1-2
Then Jonah prayed unto the Lord his God out of the fish's belly. 2nd And I cried by reason of mine affliction unto the Lord, and he heard me; out of the belly of hell cried I, and thou heard my voice.

Jesus in the heart of the earth:

Acts 2:27; BECAUSE THOU WILT NOT LEAVE MY SOUL IN HELL, NEITHER WILT THOU SUFFER THINE HOLY ONE TO SEE CORRUPTION.

Three days and three nights; the bible says Jonah was in the belly of the whale (Hebrew) sheol forever. There are three in the Godhead and they are three anointing's as I brought out earlier. There are three major feasts, three parts of the tabernacle. This is just a start here on what the number three represents. Resurrection, power and life, the same as the number seven.

11 Timothy 2:15
Study to shew thyself approved unto God, a workman that needs not to be ashamed, rightly dividing the word of truth.

So let us be the Lord's delight by always giving a just weight how? By studying (not only reading) running reference looking up the meanings of the words, keeping **Notes** and as you study. You write the verses down, as you look back months later you will see you have grown. It will amaze you, it gives you a little push to have a desire to study more.

If we plant not the truth, we are planting lies that bring not life but death, be careful where you go and what you hear, not everyone that says Lord has got the truth.

How We Know Them:

1. **They will be honest**

    Luke 8:15 (Jesus speaking)
    "But that on good ground are they, which is an honest and good heart, having heard the word, keep it, and bring forth fruit with patience"

    We hear this word it will take root in our heart and it will produce good fruit, we must water it, give it plenty of sunlight so it will bring forth life and truth, not death.

    Romans 12:17
    Recompense to no man evil for evil. Provide things honest in the sight of all men.
    Recompense (Greek) Repay.
    In other words, do not by any means to try to get even or get revenge. I know sometimes what we like to do, and what we are to do, is not always an easy thing to do sometimes. If we try to repay back what is done to us, the other person will retaliate; will cause more trouble that will lead you in

destruction. The end result could be deadly; will it be worth the price it will cost you in the end? So leave it alone put it in God's hands, he will take care of the matter.

Romans 13:10
Love works no ill to his neighbor; Therefore Love is the fulfilling of the law.

Jesus is the fulfillment of the law, he is love, he loved us enough to come to earth and shed his blood for us so that we could live.

Romans 13:13-14
Let us walk honestly, as in the day; not rioting and drunkenness, not in chambering and wantonness, not in strife and envying.
14th But put ye on the Lord Jesus Christ and make not provision for the flesh, to fulfil the lust thereof.
Rioting (Greek) Carousing, reveling
Chambering (Greek) Sexual immorality
Wantonness (Greek) Sensual, filthy

We are to keep ourselves spotless in all areas of our life. Not being drunk, to go out carousing around, fulfilling the lust of the flesh; putting on the sinful nature of Adam. We are to put on Jesus Christ and him crucified, risen and coming again. In other words let us love one another as Christ has loved us, and gave his life for our ransom.

I Corinthians 6:18-20
Flee fornication, every sin that a man does is without the body; but he that commit fornication sins against his own body.

19th What? Know ye not that your body is the temple of the Holy Ghost which is in you, which ye have of God, and ye are not your own.
20th For ye are bought with a price; therefore glorify God in your body, and your spirit which are God's

Philippians 4:8
Finally brethren, whatsoever thing are true, whatsoever things are honest, whatsoever things are just, whatsoever things are pure, whatsoever things are lovely, whatsoever things of a good report; if there be any virtue, and there be any praise, think on these things.

We are to think and meditate on honesty, truth, justice, pureness, and lovely things in the Lord. We are to give our Lord Jesus the praise and honor due him. We are to give good reports and to give the truth of his word. We must be pure in heart and give honest report always. We must walk in the truth of the Lord.

2. **There Will Be Few:**

Matthew 7:14
Because strait is the gate, and narrow is the way which leads unto life, and few there be that find it.

Matthew 9:37
Then said he unto his disciples, the harvest is plenteous, but the labors are few.

There are very few people willing to shake off the traditions of man; we are to put on the whole armor (not part of it) of God that we will be able to stand against the whiles (tricks) of the devil. We are to do the will of the Father regardless of the circumstances in our life. Walk in the way of the Lord and he will direct our path thereof. Remember our flesh is weak, our spirit is willing, for many a people started out in the way of the Lord but got weary, weak, and strayed. Remember we are to put our desires and lustful ways under subjection of the spirit, so that we do not fulfill our desires of the flesh. Flesh stinks in the nostrils of God. This does not mean we can go out and sin cause the flesh stinks in the nostrils of God. We are truly born again we have no desire to sin, our hearts desire is to please the Father.

Matthew 7:14
Because strait is the gate, and narrow is the way which leads unto life, and few there will find it.

Jesus taught that we are not to expect the majority to follow him on the road that leads to life. A few will follow through the humble gate of true repentance. Therefore deny oneself and follow one true and living God. We are to persevere until the end in all pureness to be honest in all things. To love our neighbor as our self, to walk in the righteousness of God, for we are the righteousness of God.

3. **They Will Be Calm:**

Proverbs 18:13
He that answers a matter before he hears it, folly and shame unto him.

I Corinthians 6:1
Dare any of you, having a matter against one another, go to law before the unjust and not before the saints?

What is a fair hearing? A fair hearing is hearing both sides of the story while you keep quiet. We are to give the person a chance to defend themselves. It could be a matter of misunderstanding, and it could be resolved between the two or more parties involved. We must listen whole heartedly before we act on impulse. Therefore we will not stir up anger, malice, and resentment to wound someone's spirit beyond repair. We are never to take a bro/sis before an unjust judge, in other words before the wicked Worldly system. We are to take the matter before the true loving uncondemning mature counsel of God, to weigh the matter. I am not talking if things do not pan out that we are to throw a saint away, we can ask them to leave with love till they get a better spirit.

Folly (Hebrew) foolishness, thoughtless speech.

4. **A Soft answer**:

Proverbs 15:1-4
A soft answer turns away wrath: but grievous words stir up anger.
2nd The tongue of the *wise* uses **Knowledge** aright: but the mouth of fools pours out foolishness.
3rd The eye of the Lord are in every place, beholding the evil and the good.
4th A WHOLESOME TONGUE is a TREE of LIFE: but perverseness therein is a breach in the spirit.

Proverbs 25:15
A long forbearing is a prince persuaded, a soft tongue breaks a bone.

A soft answer will keep the situation under control. There has been times an angry mother would come to my house for the children would not be getting along, I did not play into the anger, I had God to help me what to say, to keep the situation in control. And in moments God had me to calm the mother down and talk about the matter and was able to work it out. A soft answer keeps peace and understanding, bringing reconciliation in the situation, while harsh words will kill, and destroy. Harsh words in a moment of anger has destroyed and split homes churches and even businesses, in a moment of anger people has been murdered. The harsh words has caused deep rooted bitterness that is worse than cancer, it will tear down in moments what it has taken years to build, not using **Wisdom**. I have seen preachers get behind the pulpit not seasoning their words and has caused not only one person to leave and never enter another church house, but I have seen where eight people walked out; twenty years later never went back to church. It sometimes does not matter who is wrong and who is right, it is a matter to keep a soft answer and a controlled tongue, using **Wisdom** in the situation to keep it under control, Just to prove you are right is it worth being right or is it worth keeping a quiet tongue. Sometimes it is better to let the matter go, not act hastily but pray about it for an hour maybe a day, we are to weigh out the matter, I have seen this done and it works better than jumping in without **Wisdom**.

We must watch what we say especially in front of children, they are so innocent and take everything at face value. There was an incidence of a woman with her two young sons. They were to meet with sister (I will call her Blanche) from the church to have coffee at a restaurant. The young woman was running late and the oldest son asked if they were going to go pick up Sister Blanche. She said, "I don't care if we pick her up or not, she's two-faced anyhow." The one son that was red headed and quiet, the four year old, was listening to every word mommy said. Finally when they arrived to get Sister Blanche, the young red head looked at Sister Blanche and said, "Mommy, I only see one face on Sister Blanche." I cannot imagine what she felt as her four year-old exposed her in front of the woman she had talked about in front of her two sons. What that sister must have thought when the young child repeated what his mother had said about her. This undoubtedly caused a great conflict and hurt that Sister. Children are innocent and he was literally looking at her to see if she really had two faces.

Matthew 5:44
But I say unto you, love your enemies, bless them that curse you, do good to them that hate you, pray for them which despitefully use you, and persecute you.

When we love with a Godly love and love our enemies enough to pray for them, what you are doing is letting go and let God work it out, to deal with the circumstances. Also you are heaping coals of fire upon their heads. When you pray for them you are not setting yourself up to be an instrument of the enemy.

Proverbs 16:25
There is a way that seemeth right unto a man, but the end thereof are the ways of death.

We may think we are right, and we may very well be right, but proving to be right without using **Wisdom** on the situation can be very deadly to the matter. The enemy is working continually to work up strife especially in the church world. There was a time in my life as a young woman with three young children; a woman in the church was trying to come against me. Taking lies to the pastor, I ask my good friend who was one of the deacons in the church if I should take this matter to the pastor, or should I confront the Woman. He told me we should pray about the matter and let the pastor deal with the matter. The woman left the church quietly never knew what happened, did I ask? No I left it alone for God took care of the situation. Just to prove I was right, and I did nothing wrong and let the enemy use me, making the pastor feel he is not capable of taking care of the matter could have caused a lot of problems and the tables could have turned on me, and she would have gotten victory.

Proverbs 15:4
A wholesome tongue is a tree of life, but perverseness therein is a breach in the spirit.
Perverseness (Hebrew) Deceit
Breach (Hebrew) Brokenness, fainthearted, injury.

A truthful healthy tongue brings life and unity in the situation, but deceit brings injury insult and brokenness in the spirit that can bring death. We should choose our words carefully. This is not only in the church world it is this way in every situation of our life.

Its Influence is Potent:
Proverbs 15:7
The lips of the wise disperse knowledge: but the heart of the foolish doeth not so.
Disperse (Hebrew) scattered, spread out, cast away.

In other words the wise tongue spreads knowledge scatters it all around everywhere he goes. But a foolish person does not.

Proverbs 15:13
A merry heart makes a cheerful countenance; but by sorrow of the heart the spirit is broken.

Numbers 6:26
The Lord lift up his countenance upon the, and give thee peace.

The countenance is the expression of our face when we are given a good word it shows happy. When we are given a harsh word and our heart is broken, we show sadness. The Lord will give us peace love and encouragement when our spirit is broken.

Countenance (Hebrew) appearance, show of ones face, disappoint, forefront, pleased.
We must spread good cheer and love everywhere we go. We are never to sow discord among the brethren for God is not the author of confusion. God is not partakers of any rumors or Gossip, whether or not it is true we are never to condemn them, remember they still belong to God. God said in his word not to offend the least of them. They would rather be a millstone Hung about your neck to offend the least of my little ones. Remember I said earlier once you are born in this world you cannot be in anyway unborn. And I said same in the spiritual, once you are born in the spirit into the body of Christ, you cannot be unborn. That Jesus is the one time **Mediator**.

I Timothy 2:5
For there is one God, and one **MEDIATOR** between God and man, the man Christ Jesus.

Hebrews 8:6
But now hath he obtained a more excellent ministry, by how much also he is the **MEDIATOR** of a better covenant, which are established upon better promises.

I John 2:1
My little children, these things I write unto you, that ye sin not. And **IF ANY MAN SIN**, we have an **ADVOCATE** with the Father, Jesus Christ the righteous.

He can never be used again as a **Mediator**? No! Then, if we sin, we have an Advocate with the Father. When we fall or make blunders, our calling and gifts are without repentance. I am not saying to use them behind the pulpit; but do not disfellowship them. And it does not give you a right to gossip about them. We are to take them to the Lord in prayer. This cheerfulness that I am talking about will spread like wild fire. It will bring influence into the body. We are to look through the EYE of God. When he sees us he sees the blood of the Lamb.
Mediator (Greek) a go between
Advocate (Greek) intercessor, counselor, helper, comforter

We pray the Father in Jesus' name, we go to the Father for he becomes our Advocate, For Jesus made a way by being our one time Mediator, the go between God and man. That we can go to the Father as our Advocate. We can go as many times as we need and at any time of day or night.

Notes

Chapter 12

Abiding in Wisdom

Matthew 7:14
Therefore whosoever hears these sayings of mine, and doeth them, I will liken unto a man which built his house upon a Rock.

Luke 6:48
He is like a man which built an house, and dug deep, and laid the foundation on a Rock: and when the flood arose, the stream vehemently upon the house, and could not shake it, for it was founded upon the a Rock.

Matthew 16:18 (Jesus Speaking)
"And I say also unto thee, That thou art Peter, And upon this ROCK I will build my CHURCH; and the Gates of HELL (Hades) shall not prevail against it."

Jesus told Peter, to build his church on The Rock, Jesus is the Rock. Peter did not say he was building a church in his name, Peter said God told him to build his church on Jesus Christ, for he is the ROCK!
Prevail (Greek) To overcome.

Right here should have been translated Hades the place of the dead, the grave. The grave could not hold Jesus. His soul could not even be touched or see corruption. On the third appointed day (Power, Resurrection and Life) Jesus rose from the grave (**Hades**). We see the grave had no dominion over Jesus' body.

The Lord told Peter, to build his church upon the Rock the stone the builders rejected. The Chief Corner Stone from which all measurement originates. We are his lively stones. First the blueprint has to be drawn up before you can lay the foundation. God had everything drawn up before the foundation of the world was framed. He knew man would fall.

Revelation 13:8
The Lamb slain from the foundation of the world.

Genesis 3:15
And I will put enmity between thee and the woman, and between thy seed and her seed; It shall bruise thy head, and thou shalt bruise his heel.
Enmity (Hebrew) hatred, hostility.

God had the plans already laid out. This is the first recorded prophetic message.

I Corinthians 3:9-11
For we are labors together with God: ye are God's husbandry, ye are God's building.
10th According to the Grace of God which is given unto me, as a **WISE MASTER BUILDER,** I have laid the foundation, and another builds thereon. But let every man take heed how he builds thereupon.
11th For the other foundation, can no man lay than that is laid, which is ***JESUS CHRIST.***

I Peter 2:5-7
Ye also, as lively stone, are built up a spiritual house, an holy priesthood, to offer up spiritual sacrifices, acceptable to God by Jesus Christ.
6th Wherefore also it is contained in the scripture, BEHOLD (look) I lay in Sion A Chief Corner Stone, elect, precious; and he that believes on him shall not be confounded (confused)
7th Unto you therefore which believe he is precious; but unto them which be disobedient, the stone which the builder disallowed, the same is made the head of the corner.

Zechariah 10:4
Out of him came forth the corner, out of him the nail, out of him the battle bow, out of him every oppressor together.
Nail (Hebrew) tent-peg, stakes, pin, paddle
Battle Bow (Hebrew) archer, bowmen

Luke 14:28-29 (Jesus Speaking)
"For which of you, intending to build a tower, sits not down first, and count the cost, whether he have sufficient to finish it.
29th Lest haply, after he hath laid the foundation, and is not able to finish it all that behold it begin to mock him."

We must count the cost, before you start anything. We see here it will cost our life, body and soul. Are we ready to sell out, give our all, to empty ourselves, to build upon Jesus Christ, the Master Builder? When you build your house, you must dig your footer thirty two inches deep, below the freezing mark. Then you must have a chief corner stone and it must be measured correctly, no room for mistake not even off one fraction of an inch. This is the first Corner and the rest of the corners have to be crisscrossed from corner to corner, this will square it up. Then all the rest will measure up correctly. We see here the foundation, the blocks must be leveled out correctly or the whole building is off, and it will lean. This will put pressure on one side or the other more and the weight will shift causing a collapse. This must be done with a transit for horizontal measurements, to be squared up evenly. We see here the importance of balance. The balance is most critical when you start building. The building must be secured for it relies on three major things.

1. The footer must be deep enough to hold and deep enough to be under the freezing point.
2. Then you must have the Chief Corner Stone.
3. Then you must measure the rest crisscross from one another to get the square.

Ephesians 2:20-22
And are built upon the Foundation of the Apostles and Prophet, Jesus himself being the Chief corner stone;
21st In whom all the building, fitly framed together growing unto an holy temple in the Lord.
22nd In whom ye also are building together for an inhabitation of God through the spirit.
Framed (Greek) to be joined together

Apostle: Is the mouthpiece of the church, one sent to put order or keep order, or one to establish the church.
Prophet: Is the seer or the eyes of the church, one who sees in the spirit with spiritual eyes to have discernment. A prophet, as I said earlier, must prophesy. Just because you can prophesy DOES NOT MAKE YOU A PROPHET! The prophet is to inform the **Apostle**, who takes care of the matter.
Pastor: One who FEEDS the FLOCK! The one who leads and the one who is gentle. In no way is a **Pastor** to jerk around or pull,

Jesus told Peter, Feed My SHEEP! St. John 21:15; He told him three times.
Teacher: The one who shows you how to do to things and gives illustrations in order to break it down to your level. He explains it in detail and gives scriptures, and provides the references. A **Preacher** tells you that you must do it.
Evangelist: A Messenger of the good news. They preach the salvation plan, the evangelist is to go out in the highways and hedges and compel them to come in. This can be nursing homes, tent revivals, jails, prisons, street ministry.

Ephesians 4:11-15
And he gave some apostles, some prophet, and some evangelist, and some pastors and teachers.
12th For the perfecting of the saints, for the work of the ministry, for edifying of the body of Christ.
13th Till we all come in the unity of the Faith, and knowledge of the Son of God, unto a PERFECT (MATURE) man, unto the MEASURE of the stature of the fullness of Christ.
14th That we henceforth, be no more Children tossed to and fro, carried about with every wind of doctrine by the sleight of men, and cunning craftiness, whereby they lie in weight to deceive.
15th But speaking the truth in love, may grow up INTO him in all things, which is the head, even Christ.

Edifying (Greek) building, construction, strengthening, developing another person's life, through acts and words of love and encouragement.
Measure (Greek) limit, portion.
Stature (Greek) height, age, life, how great, how large, time in life.
Sleight (Greek) Trickery, cunning, craftiness.
Filled (Greek) complete

So we have a firm foundation here, **Jesus Christ the Chief Corner Stone.** We must be born again, then baptized, filled with the Holy Ghost, see here three being the balance, three parts or three stages of Salvation. We are to build upon this Rock, the five-fold ministry here. For it is for the perfecting of the Saints to come into full stature, to come to full age and not to be tricked. To know a person's cunning ways and to portion out the correct measure edifying the Kingdom of God. As we all know the church is not perfected, mature or complete, so we are running a crippled church. The church today has been established on the three fold ministry. What? Yes, the church is established on the Pastor, Teacher, Evangelist, Some churches are just the two; Pastor and evangelist. There are people that say well we do not believe in the five, then why are they using three out of five, they must believe parts. The church has to be perfected, to be complete and mature. The church has not gotten there yet. I am not saying the five-fold ministry has to be in service all time, the Evangelist travels, the Apostle travels, as well as the Prophet. The Pastor cannot do it all. The Pastor is called to feed the sheep. A pastor does not correct the church; but the Apostle corrects. The Pastor does not set the church in order; but the Apostle sets it in order. Ephesians 4:11-15.

St. John 14:2-7 (Jesus Speaking)
"In my Father's house are many mansions: if it were not so, I would have told you, I go to prepare a place for you,
3rd *And if I go and prepare a place for you I will COME AGAIN, and receive you unto myself: that where I AM, there YOU may be also!"*
6th Jesus said unto him, *"I am the way, the truth, and the life; no man comes unto the Father but by ME."*

We have many rooms in our heart that it takes a key to unlock; it takes the Holy Ghost to reveal the secret rooms or chambers to us in order for us to unlock those secret rooms. We let the Lord take up his abode in us and let him be Lord of our life. Then there will be no more secret places. To allow The Lord to come into our house; we, being the mansion where God is bringing us through the fires of refining, and to come through as gold is tried in the fires of afflictions, to learn through and by our trial by our sufferings. When Jesus ascended back to the Father, Jesus went as THE GREAT HIGH PRIEST! He took His Father's royal blood to place it upon the Mercy Seat for the atonement of our sins. Then on the Day of Pentecost He sent the comforter, the Holy Ghost back to us, He took his abode in us. When we are born again he takes his abode in our heart, He said if you abide in me, I abide in you. He took up residence and he is cleansing us from the inside out.

Malachi 3:2-3
But who may abide the day of his coming? And who shall stand when he appears? For he is like a refiner's fire, and like fuller's soap: 3rd And he shall sit as a refiner and purifier of silver: (redemption) and he shall purify the sons of Levi, and purge them as gold (divine, divinity) and silver.
Refiner (Hebrew) purge away, melt, gold –smith, silver-smith, place of smelting. Webster; to melt
Fuller (Hebrew) washed, to launder

Who can ABIDE the DAY of his COMING? NOBODY! Who can STAND when He APPEARS? NOBODY!
When he takes his abode in us, this is the day of his coming, (His first coming) he came to take us through the fires like a gold and/or a silversmith takes his product through the fires. Then Jesus washes us clean by and through his blood

I have a friend in the Lord Charlotte Torango who wrote a song it goes like this: "God is building a house where creation now dwells, these rooms are God's mansions he is delivered from shoel, (hell, hades) prepared for the ages his praises to sing, God is building a house with you and with me."

Jonah 2:1-7
Then Jonah prayed unto the Lord his God out of the fish's belly.
2nd And said I cried by reason of mine affliction unto the Lord, and he heard me; out of the belly of HELL cried I, and thou heard my voice.
6th I went down to the bottoms of the mountains; the earth with her bars was about me FOREVER
7th When my soul fainted within me I remembered the Lord: and my prayer came unto thee, into thine holy temple.
Belly (Hebrew) bowels, womb, inner person, seat of emotions.

Psalms 139:8
If I ascend up into heaven, thou art there: if I make my bed in HELL,(hades) Behold (look) thou art there.

II Corinthians 5:1-2
For we know that if our *__earthly house__* of this **Tabernacle** were dissolved, we have a building of God, an house not made with hands, eternal in the heavens.
2nd For this we groan, earnestly desiring to be clothed upon our house which is from heaven.
House (Greek) habitation, home
Building (Greek) build up, to edify, develop

John 20:17
Jesus said unto her, touch me not; for I am not YET ASCENDED to my FATHER, but I go to my brethren, and say unto them, I ascend unto my Father, and your Father, and to my God, and your God.

John 20:25-27
He told Thomas to thrust his hand into my side.

Between Mary and Thomas he ascended back to the Father to present his ultimate blood sacrifice upon the MERCY SEAT for our Atonement. When he done this he brought salvation to all the World.

Acts 1:4-5
"And being assembled together with them, commanded them that they should not depart from Jerusalem, (Jesus Speaking) but wait for the PROMISE of the FATHER, *"which"* saith he, *"ye have heard of me."*
5th *"For John truly baptized with water, but ye shall be* **BAPTIZED** *with the* **HOLY GHOST** *not many days hence."* (Jesus Speaking)

St. Luke 1:17
And he shall go before him in the spirit and power of Elias, to turn the hearts of the father to the children, and the disobedient to the **WISDOM** of the Just; to make ready a people prepared for the Lord.

Luke 7:28
For I say unto you, Among those that are born of women, there is not a greater Prophet than John the Baptist; but he that is least in the Kingdom of God is greater than he.

St. John 1:27-30
He it is, who coming after me is preferred before me, whose shoe's latchet I am unworthy to unloose.
29th The next day John sees Jesus coming unto him, and saith **"BEHOLD THE LAMB OF GOD!" (LOOK)**
Which takes away the sins of the world.

John the Baptist he looked and saw Jesus coming forth, for John was the forerunner of Jesus Christ. To prepare the people to introduce him to the Word. John said: I believe in a very loud voice; Look! BEHOLD The LAMB of GOD! Here is Jesus the one who will take away our sins and give us life.

Jesus came to make atonement for our sins. The Past, Present, Future, to be covered and washed in the Blood of the Lamb.

I Peter 4:17
For the time is come that judgment must began at the house of God: and if it first began at us, what shall the end be of them that obey not the gospel of God.

When we are born again Jesus takes his abode in the heart of our mind, for judgment begins at the house of God.

II Peter 1:19
And the Day Star shines in a dark place (within us) until the Day dawn, and the Day Star arises in your hearts.

I Peter 2:5
We are lively stones built up a spiritual house to Jesus Christ being the Chief Corner Stone.

Hebrews 10:19-21
Having therefore brethren, boldness to enter into the holiest by the blood of Jesus.
20th By a NEW and LIVING WAY, which he hath consecrated for us, through the veil, that is to say his flesh.
21st And having an High Priest over the house of God (us, house).

Having Jesus our Great High Priest over and in our house, the day he took his abode in us.

I Corinthians 6:19-20
What? Know ye not that your body is the temple of the Holy Ghost which is in you, which ye have of God, and you are not your own?
20th For ye are BOUGHT with a PRICE: Therefore glorify God in your body. And in your spirit, which are God's

Hebrews 9:11-13
But Christ being come an High Priest of good things to come, by a greater more perfect tabernacle (Not of wood Buildings) not made by hands, that is to say, not of this building.
12th Neither by the blood of Goats and calves, but by his OWN BLOOD he entered in ONCE into the Holy Place, having obtained eternal redemption for us.
13th For if the blood of bulls and goats, and the ashes of an heifer sprinkling the unclean, sanctifies to the purifying of the flesh:

Jeremiah 28:23
Am I a God at hand, says the Lord, and had not a God afar off?

You see where I am coming from now? WE DO NOT SERVE A FAR OFF GOD! The Great High Priest, Jesus Christ dwells within the heart of our mind. He is burning out all the dross, bringing us through the fires of redemption. Bringing us through the fire as the Hebrew boys were thrown into the fires they had their ropes burned off no longer bound in bondage of man. We are the gold tried in the fire. We are his mansions, we are the many rooms, it takes many rooms to make a mansion. He is building with you and with me. For where he is there we may be also, this took place on the Day of Pentecost. He is molding us back into

His image before the fall of man. The only thing different we will have went full circle.

Ephesians 2:6
And he raised us up together and made us sit together in heavenly places in Christ Jesus

We can sit in heavenly places; but we do not have to die in order to obtain the riches of our heavenly Father. We can obtain here. First we must seek so we can find his unsearchable riches. We are to seek ye first the kingdom of heaven and all his righteousness, our hearts should want nothing but the fullness of the Lord. To seek for all he has for us, it is his good pleasure to give us his kingdom.

I Corinthians 2:9-10
But it is written, eye hath not seen, nor heard, neither have entered into the heart of man, the things which God hath prepared for them that love him.
10th **BUT GOD HATH REVEALED THEM** unto us by **HIS SPIRIT!** for the spirit searches all things, yea the deep things of God.

Colossians 1:26
Even the mystery which has been hid from the ages and from generations, but now is made manifest to his saints.

So God is revealing to us the things he has prepared for us, we do not have to die to obtain these treasures. God reveals them by the Holy Ghost. These deep things are treasures of his pure word, not doctrine of men. How can the church teach us when the secular church is crippled? They have traditions of men handed down by their fore-fathers instead of the truth of God?

Colossians 1:26
Even the mystery which has been hid from the ages and from the generations, but now is made manifest to his saints:

So God is revealing to us the things he has prepared for us. We do not have to die to obtain these treasures. God reveals them by the Holy Ghost. These deep treasures are treasures of his pure word, not doctrine of men. How many have been taught by the Holy Ghost? In other words, we should be getting in the word, studying, running references, and studying out the Old Testament; taking it to the New Testament. I hear people say they studied with the best men. I am studying with the best, The Holy Ghost, he is the teacher.

Colossians 1:13-16
Who hath delivered us from the power of darkness, and hath translated us into the Kingdom of his dear Son.
14th In whom we have redemption through his blood, even the forgiveness of sins:
15th Who is the image of the firstborn of every creature:
16th For by him were all things created, that are in heaven, and that are in earth visible and invisible, whether they be thrones, or dominions or principalities or powers: All things were created by him and for him.

I Corinthians 6:19
What? Know ye not that ye are the temple of the Holy Ghost which is in you, which ye have of God, and ye are not your own?

Isaiah 9:6
For unto us a child is born, unto us a son is given; and the government shall be upon his shoulder;

Ephesians 4:15-16
But speaking the truth (gospel) in love, may grow up in all things, which is the head, even Christ.
16th From whom the WHOLE BODY fitly joined together and compacted by which every joint supplies, according to the effectual working in the measure of every part, makes increase of the body unto edifying of itself in love.

Colossians 1:18
And he is the **HEAD** of the **BODY,** the **Church**; Who is the beginning, the firstborn from the dead, that in all things he might have the preeminence.
Preeminence (Greek) To be supreme, first-place, first
Gate (Greek) Entrance to a city, gateway, porter

I Peter 2:9
But ye are a **CHOSEN GENERATION, A ROYAL PRIESTHOOD, AN HOLY NATION, A PECULIAR PEOPLE**:
That he should shew forth the praises of him who hath called you out of darkness into his marvelous light:

Revelation 1:6
And hath made us KINGS and PREIST unto God and his Father; to him be glory and dominion for ever and ever, Amen.

Revelation 5:10
And hast made us unto our God KINGS and PRIEST: And we shall reign on the Earth.

We see in the scriptures here he is perfecting his body, making his body mature and complete in Him. Then he will have a place to lay his head upon the shoulder (strength). God is building His house, built with **Wisdom** with the revelation, in the Knowledge, which is established with understanding. We see here we do not serve a far off God! He took up his abode in us the day we were born again. He took up residence he rules and reigns from our heart. We do not pray way up in the heaven, we do not need to scream, holler, or yell to get his attention, he lives inside of us. He is our Great High Priest that lives within our very being. He is in the Holy of Holies, (the heart of our mind) where he applied the blood upon the Mercy seat.

We are not only the chosen generation! We are the Priesthood, we are the Holy Nation, we are the Lord's possession, we are his own we were bought with a price. We were bought by and through the precious royal blood of Jesus. We are called by his name, he gave us his power, for we are his BODY! We are no longer in darkness, he is put his light in us the moment we were born again for he is the light within us. We are to praise him now, and throughout eternity.

Peculiar (Greek) ones very own, special, possession, purchased.

Genesis 1:27
So God Created Man In His Own Image, in the Image of God created He Him; Male and Female;

Genesis 2:7
And the Lord God Formed Man of the Dust of the Ground, and Breath into his nostrils the breath of life, and the man became a living SOUL!

Life is in the Blood!
The created man is the Spirit man, The Formed man is the soul (**soulish**) man. The created man has to go back into the formed man to make one new man.

Two Natures

Galatians 5:9-23
A little leaven leaveneth the whole lump.
22nd But the fruit of the spirit is love, joy, peace, longsuffering, gentleness, goodness, faith,
23rd Meekness, temperance against there is no law.
Romans 5:16-21
And not as it was by one that sinned, so is the gift; for the was by one to condemnation, but the free gift is of many offences unto justification.
17th For if by one man's offence death reigned by one; much more they which receive abundance of grace and the gift of righteousness shall reign in life by one, Jesus Christ.
21st That as sin hath reigned unto death, even so might Grace reign through righteousness unto eternal life by Jesus Christ our Lord.

Old Nature	*New Nature*
The first Adam was earthy made of the ground, (Fleshly) Old Man – Death	Second Adam from Heaven, the Spirit of man-Jesus New Man: Life, Ephesians 4:24
Adultery, fornication, uncleanness, Lasciviousness, Idolatry, Witchcraft, Hatred, Variance, Emulations, Wrath, Strife	Love, joy, peace, longsuffering, gentleness, goodness, faith, meekness, temperance
Seditions, Heresies	God is Love – Agape
Ishmael/Bondswoman Hagar	Isaac/Freewoman Sarah
Two eyes/see double/flesh	Eye/Single-full of light/The eye of God
Condemnation/Death	Justification/Life

/Law	Grace/Righteousness
Circumcision/Flesh	Circumcision/Heart
Slave/Servant	Son/Free
Darkness/Lies	Light/Truth
Lust of the Flesh/Eyes, pride of life	Redemption
The Old Nature **CANNOT UNDERSTAND** God I Corinthians 1:18	New Nature **UNDERSTANDS** God Ephesians 2:15
The Old Nature **CANNOT OBEY** God Ephesians 2:2	New Nature **OBEYS** God Romans 6:3-7 & 2 Corinthians 5:17
CANNOT SERVE TWO MASTERS Matthew 6:24	There is **ONE TRUE GOD** I Corinthians 8:6

Notes

Chapter 13

Changes Made in us by Wisdom

Tabernacle

Three Parts of the Tabernacle

1. **The Outer Court:**

Or the Courtyard is the blood atonement of Christ. The only means of light was the sun, represents the body of man. This is **Passover;** this is the first anointing, this is the thirty- fold Christian. This is **gate (Thanksgiving)** of the white linen fence which is the righteousness of the Saints; into the place of sacrifice, where the priests are sacrificing and where the blood is shed. Where they are to go through the blood; and where they are forgiven. This is a place of repentance, a place of forgiveness. This is the good will.

Romans 12:2
And be not conformed to this world; be ye transformed by the renewing of your mind that ye may prove what is that good, and acceptable, and perfect will of God.

2. **The Holy Place:**

   Where the soul is brought into submission, this is Pentecost, the Feast of Pentecost and first-fruits. This is the sixty-fold Christian the silver vessel, our redemption, where they we enter into the Door (Jesus) where they come into the realm of Pentecost, the second anointing, where they are filled with the Holy Ghost. This is called the Holy Place, the place of praise.

   A. Where the lampstand is at the south side, it is to your left when you enter into the Holy Place. The lampstand was one piece of gold beaten from an entire talent weighing seventy five pounds. They are set in place as they shed light to the front. They are wick trimmers who trimmed or pruned back the wicks so the lamps will burn brighter, if not the lamps got blackened and you could not see the flame burn. Every-time they trimmed the lamps they had to put in more oil, or incense in the bowls. The lampstand represents the Holy **Spirit** (Hebrew) Holy **Ghost** (Greek) his was the only means of light for there were no windows in the sanctuary, not a natural light but an inward light. The light was provided by the seven lamps made of gold. Jesus representing the shaft holding three bowls on each side. Shaft means the thigh, body or side. Three is the same as seven and also means resurrection power and life. Type of Christ, seven symbolizes divine perfection. The size of the lampstand is about five foot tall by three and a half feet wide. The candlestick represents Jesus the Baptizer, the seven spirits of God. The candlestick represents the outpouring of the Holy Ghost, and power, Acts 2:1-4. The costly oil, Myrrh, sweet cinnamon, sweet calamus, cassia bound with the olive oil. The standard of the sanctuary, one hin of olive oil blended all together makes five which represents Grace of God. **This is Priestly/ Kingly Anointing!** This is where we will rule and reign, the second sealing (Holy Ghost) This is the **acceptable** will of God. Romans 12:2; this is the praise and worship realm, this is Word and spirit. This is where the soul is brought into submission.

B. **The table of Shew Bread:**

Shew-bread (Hebrew) food, bread of presence, feast, show ones face in other words we eat the bread of life, he is our life we will see the face of God. This is the first-fruits. This is the second piece of furniture in the Holy Place

Hebrews 9:2
For there was a tabernacle made; the first, wherein was the candlestick, and the table, and the showbread; which is called the sanctuary.

Matthew 12:4
How he entered into the house of God, and did eat the showbread, which was not lawful for him to eat, neither for them which were with him, but only for the priests?

The table is made of acacia wood is overlaid with pure gold and made a molding of gold around it. The table of showbread was crowned twice, it points to Jesus Christ the Son of God, Jesus the Son of Man Jesus being crowned Lord of lords and King of kings: they are two crowning's here. Two cubits was its length, a cubit was it breadth, and a cubit and a half of its height. The only piece of furniture in its height that was equal to the Ark. The bread of life and the golden altar of incense are where our will is ground down, our will submitted to the Holy Ghost through our sacrifice of praise. This is act of Worship. This altar represents our human emotions, where our will is submitted to the Holy Ghost. There is twelve loaves of bread, two stacks, six in each stack two meaning union, six the number of man and his fleshly/beastly nature. Twelve means divine law and order and, this represents the Bread of Life (Jesus). The High Priest is to partake of the showbread, the bread represents Jesus Christ's body, who is the first-fruit of them that slept, and the first-fruit of our redemption.

3. **The Holy of Holies:**

Or the Most Holy Place: The Spirit: This is Tabernacle; this is where we come into the very Presence of God. This is the GLORY REALM! The Lord told me it is time for his people to enter into the Tabernacles; time has come for the veil (to be rent from top to bottom) to be lifted off our eyes, This is the 100 fold Christian, this is the full mature/perfect and complete man where there Is no flesh, not schism, this is where the high priest dwells; where the Shekinah Glory of God come down to consume our sacrifice, no longer I that lives but Christ in me the hope of glory. Where the body becomes one in unity, no more division; where Christ can lay his head upon his Shoulders (government) the body is complete, to have matured to perfection. This is WORSHIP, WHERE The GLORY of God FLOWS! This is healing, where we are made whole; this is the secret place. This is where prayers are answered (We only enter this in moments at a time). We will enter one finale time and never leave. This is Harvest time, time of the gathering. Hebrews 9:1-28; read the whole chapter if you can. This is fullness of the spirit, this is where our inheritance is granted to us. This is not just worship this is worship in spirit and in truth where the GLORY REALM IS! This eternal salvation, a point of no return. This is the **PERFECT WILL** OF THE FATHER, the divine life. This is the third anointing the third sealing of the saints, the golden vessel tried in the fire. This is the place where the baptism of fire is, this is where we become one with God, As Jesus said me and my Father are ONE, so Are We! As He is so are we. We are pleasing to the Great High Priest! We become the living sacrifice. We are under total surrender of the Lordship of Jesus Christ. This is where we totally recognize God the Father in every aspect of our Lives. Revelation 5:9-10.

A. ***The Mercy Seat:***
The Mercy Seat Is the Work of Christ. The Mercy Seat is higher than the ark (law) the ministry of death. God gave the law to expose man's sin.

B. ***The Ark of The Covenant:***
It is overlaid in gold and made from Shittim wood.
1. This represents the THRONE Of GOD!
2. This represent the person of Jesus Christ, the fullness of God!
3. This represents the presence of God.
4. This represents the glory of God.
5. This represents the life of God
6. The Gold within, middle, outside
7. Located in the Most Holy Place.

Inside The Ark:
Aaron's rod that budded; the Ten Commandments, and the manna.
When the Ark was opened the reason the person died that he was not the High Priest, it opened up the law of sin and death. Only the high priest could touch the ark. Also the Ark can also mean a coffin.

Romans 12:1-2
I beseech you brethren by the mercies of God, that you present your bodies a living sacrifice, holy and acceptable unto God, which is your reasonable service.
Beseech (Greek) plead, encourage, urge, comfort, to beg, to pray
Acceptable (Greek) well pleasing, accepted.

What it is saying here is: I encourage and plead or beg with you, to give your mind, body and soul to God Almighty to give your all. He wants a live sacrifice not a dead sacrifice. He wants your love, your devotion and your life, to love him with all your heart, mind, and soul. He wants to be Lord in all aspects of your life. For you to sell out to do what he has called you to be and do, **A Vessel of Honor!**
Conformed (Greek) Pattern, mold or fashion.
Transformed (Greek) Changed, transfigured, change in form.

Do not let the world mold you, do not pattern after the ways of the world, but let God change you. How? By the washing of the Word. What do you mean washing of the Word? When we open up our Bible and not only read it, but study it, we are eating the word. What is the difference in reading the bible and studying the bible? When we read the bible which is ok, it is just reading it more like a regular book. But when you read a verse stop there, if you have a middle column with scriptures they have letters, in your verse you just read should have a letter beside one of the words. Then you take the letter in your verse, go to the middle column, you will find one or more letters in the column that matches, go to the scripture it tells you, it will give you more on the scriptures. Then get you a bible dictionary or a concordance to look up the meanings of the words. Anytime there is a translation into another language sometimes it takes two to four words to substitute a word. This word when we study it begins to digests into our bellies where it starts to get bitter; this is where the washing begins in us. This is where we begin to grow and the weeds get choked out. This is where we decrease and God increases. He wants us to be in his PERFECT WILL!

II Timothy 2:21
If a man therefore purge himself from these, he shall be a **vessel of honor**, sanctified, and meet for the Master's use. And prepared unto every good work.

James 4:7
Submit yourselves therefore to God, Resist the devil and he will flee from you.
8th Draw nigh to God, and he will draw nigh to you, cleanse your hands, ye sinners; and purify you hearts, ye double minded.
Purge (Greek) Cleanse, get rid of
Submit (Greek) Subjection, obedient
Draw (Greek) Come near, near, approaching
Vessel (Greek) Useful, helpful, serviceable, profitable
Meet (Greek) useful, helpful, serviceable, profitable

We are to purge ourselves, to cleanse ourselves from all unrighteousness. To rid anything in our heart or life that does not pertain to God. We must put ourselves under subjection to be obedient to the Holy Ghost. To draw nigh is to approach God with a sincere heart to draw near him. We are to be a vessel unto him, for him to possess us, for us to be useful, to be of service unto him profitable unto his will.

Ephesians 6:5
Servants, be obedient to them that are your masters according to the flesh, with fear, and trembling, in singleness of heart, as unto Christ.

Hebrews 10:22
Let us draw near with a true heart in full assurance of faith, having our hearts sprinkled from an evil conscience, and our bodies washed pure with water.
Washed (Greek) bathed

So here we see he does not want us to just get our feet wet, or just to pour water on us. He wants us to be submerged totally; to bathe is to get our whole bodies in water to get soaked. He wants us saturated. This is spiritual cleansing.

Romans 6:3-8
Know ye not, that so many of us were baptized **into** Jesus Christ were baptized into his death?
4th Therefore we are buried with him by baptism into death: that like as Christ was raised up from the dead by the glory of the Father, even so we should walk in the newness of life.
5th For if we have been planted together in the likeness of his death, we shall be also in the likeness of his resurrection.
8th Now if we be dead with Christ, we believe that we shall also live with him.

II Corinthians 7:1
Having therefore these promises, dearly beloved, let us cleanse ourselves from all filthiness of the flesh and spirit, perfecting holiness in the fear of God.

We are a vessel here and we must keep our vessels dipped in water (Washing of the Word) then apply oil to the vessel. When we apply the oil to smear the vessel, it has to be smeared or rubbed in vigorously. The vessel here that it is talking about is made of leather, the leather gets brittle and it will crack if it is not dipped in water and rubbed in oil. We the people represent a vessel that must be watered, (The Word) then smeared in oil (Holy Ghost) or we will get brittle and our vessels will crack, then our oil will leak out.

Acts 9:15
But the Lord said unto him, (Jesus Speaking) *"Go thy way: for he is chosen vessel unto me, to bear my name before the Gentiles, and kings, and the children of Israel."*

Proverbs 25:3-4
The heaven for height and the earth for depth, and the heart of kings is unsearchable.
4th Take away the dross from the silver, and there shall come forth a vessel for the finer.

Hebrews 7:26-28
For such an high priest became us, who is holy, harmless, undefiled, separate from sinners, and made higher than the heavens.
27th Who needs not daily, as those high priests, to offer up sacrifice, first for his own sins, and made higher than the heavens.

28th For the law makes men high priest which have infirmity; but the word of oath, which was since the law, makes the Son, who is consecrated for evermore.

Hebrews 10:19-23
Having therefore, brethren, boldness to enter into the holiest by the blood of Jesus.
20th By a new and living way, which he hath consecrated for us, through the veil, that is to say, his flesh;
21st And having a high priest, over the house of God.
22nd Let us draw near with a true heart in full assurance of faith, having our hearts sprinkled from evil
conscience, and our bodies washed in pour water.
23rd Let us hold fast the profession of our faith without wavering; **(for he is faithful)**.
Consecrated (Greek) Dedicate, inaugurate, to perfect, completed, finish

I believe what it is saying here; under the law the high priest has to offer up a sacrifice for himself, for his own sins, then he was able to offer up sacrifices for the people. Once a year this had to be done it did not cover the sins, it pushed them back one more year. Then Jesus who knew no sin, came little lower than the angels, in a form of a servant, took our sins upon himself nailing them to the cross. Offering his sacrificial blood to pour upon the Mercy seat once and for all.
High Priest (Hebrew) Who not only has religious duties, but he also had to examined people and things for medical diagnosis, policed the unruly, and taught the word of God, chief rulers.

Isaiah 53: 3-12

He is despised and rejected a man of sorrows acquainted with grief: and we hid as it were our faces from him; he was despised, and we esteemed him not.

4th Surely he hath borne our grief, and carried our sorrows: yet we esteemed him stricken, smitten of God, and afflicted.

5th But he was wounded for our transgressions, he was bruised for iniquities: the chastisement of our peace was upon him; and with his stripes we are healed.

10th Yet it pleased the Lord to bruise him; he hath put him to grief: when thou shalt make his soul an offering for sin, he shall see his seed, he shall prolong his day, and the pleasure of the Lord shall prosper in his hand.

11th He shall see of the travail of his soul, and shall be satisfied: by his knowledge shall my righteous servant justify many.

12th Therefore will I divide him a portion with the great, and he was numbered with the transgressors; and bare the sin of many, and made intercession for the transgressors.

Jesus, being our Great High Priest; Jesus taking the stripes for our healing. The bible does not say how many stripes Jesus took. It does tells how many Apostle Paul took forty save one, which is 39 stripes. The Jew gave 39 stripes, the Roman's gave more than 39 stripes. Jesus was beaten beyond recognition, Paul was not. Not only was Jesus beaten beyond recognition, he took a stripe for every major disease including sin and sickness. He came to those in need of a physician.

Notes

Chapter 14

Wisdom to Know When to Move, to Stand still and When to Speak

Timing is of The Essence

The Book of Esther:

Esther 2:1-23
After these things, when the wrath of King Ahasuerus was appeased, he remembered Vashti, and what was decreed against her.
3rd And let the King appoint officers in all the provinces of his kingdom, that they may gather together all the fair young virgins unto Shu'shan the palace, to the house of the women unto the custody of He'ge the King's chamberlain, keeper of the women; and let their things for purification be given them:
4th And let the maiden which pleases the king to be queen instead of Vash'ti. And the thing pleased the king; and he did so.
5th Now in Shu'shun the palace there was a Jew, who name was Mordecai, the son of Jair, the son of Shimei, the son of Kish a Benjaminite;
7th And he brought up Hadassah, that is Esther, His Uncle's Daughter: for she has neither father nor mother, and the maid was fair and beautiful; who Mordecai, when her father and

mother were dead, took for his **OWN DAUGHTER**. (Mordecai was her cousin).

8th so it came to pass, when the King's commandment and his decree was heard, and when many maidens were gathered together unto Shunshan the palace, to the custody of Hegai, keeper of the women.

9th The maiden pleased him, and she obtained kindness of him; and he speedily gave her things for purification, with such things as belonged to her, and seven (perfection, Mature, Completion) maidens, which were to meet to be given her, out of the king's house: and he preferred her and her maids unto the best of the house of the women.

10th Esther had not shewed her people nor her kindred; for Mordecai had charged her that she should not shew it.

Esther 1:10-19

Queen Vash'ti was brought before the King the royal crown, for the king to show off her beauty but the Queen refused to come at the king's command. As we see here it looks like Vash'ti the queen had a rebellious spirit, and would not listen or heed to the King. It was said she not only refused the king's command but she did wrong to all the princes, and all the people, being a bad influence to all the women toward their husbands. The King Ahasuerus; commanded Queen Vash'ti to be brought in before him, she again refused. This was all in the work of the Lord. The King said let it be written among the laws of Persians and the Medes that her royal estate be given to another better than she is. God used He'ge the King's Chamberlain to let the king choose the maiden by letting the maiden please him. Let the king appoint officers in all the provinces of his kingdom that they gather all the fair young virgins unto Shushan the palace. There was Esther, a Jew, her cousin Mordecai who raised her as his own daughter for she was orphaned, probably at a young age. So Mordecai told Esther she was the one to save her people and not let no one knew she was a Jew, not even to her own people. So Mordecai brought Esther to the palace with the other maidens into the custody of Hegai for he was the keeper of the women. Mordecai kept a close eye on Esther; watched over her kind of like at a distance but yet close. There is six months with oil of myrrh, six months of sweet odors or aromas, with other things, there is preparation time in Jewish wedding that takes at least twelve months to prepare I do not believe that this is a coincidence, God is a God of timing.

The time has come when every maiden was given whatsoever she desired, and the young maidens were brought before the King. The maidens were only brought before the King once unless the king delighted in her. Now came time for Esther to be brought before the king, she desired nothing but what Heg'ai the king's chamberlain the keeper of the women appointed. Esther obtained favor from all who saw her. The King saw Esther and not only found favor with the king, he loved her. He chose her from among all the young fair maidens, no doubt there were hundreds of young girls. She obtained Grace and favor more than any other maiden in the palace. When he found favor in Esther he placed the crown upon her head and made her queen in the palace of Vash'ti.

The king made a great feast unto all his princes and his servants, even Esther's feast; and made a release to the provinces, he gave gifts according to the state of the king. Esther still has kept her kindred to herself as she was commanded by her cousin Mordecai; Mordecai was setting at the king's gate he saw that Bigthan and Teresh were against the king and planned to lay hands on the king, so Mordecai told Esther, and Esther told the king. She told the king Mordecai told her about it. The king had an inquisition done and found it to be true, the king had them hung on a tree.

The king Ahasuerus promoted Haman to the seat above all princes that were with him. The king commanded all his servants that were within the gate to bow and reverence Haman. Mordecai refused to bow and the king noticed it. The king's servant asked Mordecai why he did not bow as the king commanded. Then Haman figured out Mordecai was a Jew for he sent servant to watch and report all they see, and he was full of wrath for Mordecai, for he would not do as he commanded. So he sought to destroy all the Jews throughout all the land. So Haman went to the king; told him all about Mordecai and how he was a Jew and their laws were different than their laws and it would not profit the king to put up with this race of people. So Haman was out to have all the Jew destroyed. But little did Haman know God already was ahead of him and God had a plan. He even bribed the king by telling him he would give him ten thousand talents of silver to the ones who does this charge of the business, to bring the money to the king's treasuries. The king took off his ring and gave it to Haman as a token. The king was all for Haman for he believed in him.

As we see here the devil is on the rampage thinking he has everything under control. He thinks he has Mordecai right where he wants him. Well little does he know God is a head of him and he knows everything the devil is thinking, planning and plotting: The devil has no clue what God is doing and God has better plans in motion. God sets them in, God set the down, and not knowing that Haman is being used of God.

The letters were sent out into all the Kings' provinces, to destroy all the Jews, men, woman, and children. The twelfth month (Adar) thirteenth day which take them as prey. When Mordecai heard what was done he rent his clothes and put on sackcloth with ashes and cried loud and with bitterness. Can you imagine knowing the very day that will seal your doom? This would make anyone cry out to God in a bitter voice. You know that we would cry out to asking: Why God: Why Lord? Did you bring us this far just to forsake us? For we are only human.

Esther heard her cousin was wroth (**angry, enraged**) and clothed in sackcloth (**course cloth worn for mourning**) with ashes. She sent raiment to clothe her cousin Mordecai, he refused the raiment that Esther sent for him to wear. Esther sent for Hatach, one of the king's chamberlains that was to attend to her, to seek out what was going on with her cousin, for she knew something was wrong for him to refuse her garments. Hatach went to see Mordecai, to check out what was going on, for Esther sake. Mordecai sent with Hatach copy of the writing of the decree (report, letter, sentence, command) that was given at Shu'shan to destroy them to his adopted daughter Esther to see. Mordecai put the whole thing in Esther's lap He sent a message that she is to go to the king's chambers to talk to him to make a request before him to save her people. Esther did not have to go to the king to talk to him if she was a very selfish and evil woman, for no one knew she was a Jew. Esther knew once she went to the king to talk with the king she would reveal who she really is. Mordecai commanded Esther to respond and not to think about herself, for she can escape; her people cannot. Esther sent word to Mordecai to gather all the Jews together in one place, tell them not to drink or eat for THREE days, (Resurrection life, power same as seven). And three nights, I and my maids will do the same (she prophesied here). I will go to the king which is not under the law, **I will save my people. Esther was appointed for such a time as this.** Mordecai went his way, to tell his people they are too fast for three days and three nights, I believe he told them Like this; My people I come to you with a heavy heart, to tell you too fast food and drink for three days and nights. This is very critical, if you do not listen and fast not to eat even one morsel of food or drink, one sip could cost our lives. Can you see the pattern here? Jonah in the belly of the whale, three days and three nights, as Jesus was in the heart of the Earth (hell) three days and three nights, there is **redemption**, there is **salvation**, there is life. I gave this throughout this book to glean from the pages here.

The third day Esther put on her royal apparel (Royal Robe of Righteousness) and went to the inner court (courtyard where the sacrifice is made) and she stood against the king's house. The king saw her standing in the inner court (within) while he was setting on the throne (seat, place of authority, seat of honor; royalty or deity) The king looked (behold) he saw her in all her beauty, she had found favor in his sight. (God is Working) The king held out to Esther the queen the golden Scepter (staff) that was in his hand. (as Moses held out his staff over the sea to part the waters). The king asked Esther what she wanted, that she could have everything up to half his kingdom.

The king asked Esther what is thy request? Esther knew when to speak, when to move. She stood at the inner court purposely for the king to see her. Then Esther moved when she knew she found favor with the king. Esther knew it was time (Timing is of the ESSENCE) to save her people. When the king asked her what her request was, that she could have anything she wanted up to half of his kingdom, for she had found favor with the king, and he loved her (symbolic to the LORD). Then Esther answered the king; if it pleased the king I want Haman (enemy) and you to come to the banquet that I have prepared (See where **Wisdom** builds her house, she prepares the banquet table) for him. She has already started to speak in **Wisdom**, knowledge and understanding. She is going forth with caution, waiting to hear (incline) from the Lord when to move. The king granted Esther her request. At the banquet of wine (spirit) the king asked Esther what her petition was and to make it know to him, and he will grant her petition. Esther made known unto the king not only her petition but her request also. If I find favor with the king, and it pleased the king to grant my petition (demand) and perform my request (desire) also. If I find favor with the king, and it please the king to grant my petition and perform my request let it be. She did not tell the king what her petition was and she asked him and he granted it to her before he knew what it was. Haman came to the banquet all smiles (lol) till he found Mordecai at the king's gate he was very Wroth, (Mordecai was wroth the tables are turning) but he refrained himself. Haman went home rejoicing, calling in all his friends to come for him and his wife had great riches and the king promoted him to high ranks above all the rest. We see here he thought he had everything under control, Is this not like the devil? And no one could touch him. He was so happy that he was so favored, to be the only one allowed by Esther and the king to be at the banqueting table. Little did he know he was being setup or being revealed be sure your sins will find you out. He had no **Wisdom**, he had false hope, he was bragging opening his mouth like a fool does (Remember the fool; the minute he opens his mouth he reveals himself). He was bragging he was to go again to the banquet table for he was invited by Queen Esther, and the king, he liked her, but he did not have a clue who she is. So Haman told his friends to make gallows for Mordecai to be hung on for he was surly going to die for Haman set this all in order for he thought he was in control.

The scene changes here:
That night the king rose up out of bed for he could not sleep. He was deep in thought no doubt, for he called on them to bring the book of records (book of life) of Chronicles to him. He asked them what honor was given to Mordecai for saving him from the two chamberlains, Bigthana and Teresh. There was not anything done in honor of Mordecai saving the kings life. Haman thinks he has got it all under control, he is at home sleeping like a baby, for he has conquered it all, having the Jews and Mordecai destroyed. But the tables are in the process of turning. The king realizing Haman is up to no good. The king sent for his chamberlains to go to Haman and bring him back to the banquet that Esther had prepared for him. The king asked Esther what petition and request she wanted and he would grant it. Esther was given full control and I believe she stood up from the table she went forth and revealed Haman and all that he is to the king that he was evil. She had proof. Can you imagine one moment the look on Haman's face? He was speechless, in horror, He realized who Esther is here; A JEW! Oh my goodness what have I done, the king says too late your life is over you are done. Haman was hung upon the gallows instead of Mordecai.

As we see the pages unfold before our very eyes what the devil meant for evil God turned it all around for the good. When we stand still and see the salvation of the Lord work. Esther, how we see such **Wisdom** and the knowledge she was given by God, to understand when she was to move. She not only had to wait but not be still, she had to gain evidence she had to be given instruction not from man but from God. She had walk in faith take a step at a time, to know the heart of God. Not only her to be destroyed but all her people. I believed there were a lot of Jews there that was saved for she was a Woman of great **Wisdom**, strength and beauty. Hosea 4:6; says: my people are destroyed for the lack of knowledge. Esther was appointed and reserved for such a time as this.

We have seen the devil can destroy you if you let him. We see where Esther and Mordecai could have thrown up their hands and say we are going to not make it loose faith and die. But Mordecai saw a way out, God revealed it to him, he saw where God was showing him Esther had the key to the kingdom. We see the portrait of Christ throughout the pages here. How we see the New Testament unfolding in the Old Testament. Always look to the Lord for he is our strength, he will fight our battles, but we must go forth in the name of the Lord to conquer. He gives us strength and **Wisdom** if we will just be quiet and listen.

Notes

Chapter 15

The Hidden Treasures of Wisdom

Isaiah 28:13
But the word of the Lord was unto them precept upon precept, precept upon precept: Line upon line; line upon line; here a little, there a little that they may go, and fall backward, and be broken, and snared, and taken.
Line (Hebrew) Ruler, measuring line
Precept (Hebrew) Commandments, law, ordinances, order

Isaiah 28: 16-17
Therefore thus said the Lord God, Behold (look) I lay in Zion for a foundation a stone, a tried stone, a precious corner Stone, a sure foundation; he that believes shall not make haste.
17th Also will I lay to the line and the righteousness to the plummet: and the hail shall sweep away the refuge of lies and the water shall overflow the hiding place.

We see here precept upon precept, which means commandments upon commandments, or law upon the law, order upon order here. Line upon line meaning measuring upon measuring, ruler upon ruler, which is showing the importance of measurements. The importance of order, there must be order, instruction, and timing. Everything MUST be Precise, it must be measured from the first corner, The Corner Stone, then it will come out

balanced a perfect measure. The foundation will be a sure foundation tried and true. The foundation will be established and the instruction **Wisdom** that has been corrected and taught throughout scriptures, rightly dividing the word of truth.
Plummet (Hebrew) Plum line, a leveling instrument.
Foundation (Hebrew) Establish, ordain, the foundation stone, sure foundation

Jeremiah 32:33
They have turned unto me the Back, and not the Face: though I taught them, rising up early and teaching them, yet they have not hearkened to receive instruction.

It goes without saying; turn our faces to the Lord, not our backs. Give him the praise and honor due him. He will bless us and cause us to mature, to love him as a son would love his father. God is our Heavenly Father ABBA! which means Daddy. He wants us not only turn our faces to him, but get in his lap to talk to him to wrap your arms around his neck, let him know he is loved as he loves you. When we are children when we are in his lap we are telling him all about our wants, our hurts and our desires, it is all about us, as we mature into adults we begin to think of our Father, what can we do for you Daddy? This is a true sign of maturity. But we have turned our backs on him; we have turned away from the teachings of the Father. We no longer hear the instructions he has given to the church. We have turned a deaf ear, no wonder the church is in the shape it is in. Judgment begins in the house of God, Judgment begins within us. We were in bondage under the law of sin and death, it is punishable by death it is condemnation. We are already condemned, punished, lost and undone, without the Lord in our hearts. We are no longer under the law of sin and death we are under Grace, which bring life.

II Peter 1:5-7
And beside this, giving all diligence, add to your faith virtue knowledge.
6th And to knowledge, temperance; and to temperance patience, and to patience godliness.
7th And to godliness brotherly kindness charity.
Virtue (Greek) goodness, excellence, moral, praises.
Temperance (Greek) self-control
Patience (Greek) endurance, enduring, waiting
Charity (Greek) **Agape** the active love of God for his son and his people. And the active love his people are to have for God; love feast, the common meal shared by Christians, feasts of charity.
Diligence (Greek) zeal, eagerness, haste, carefulness, hurry, earnestly

We see here that we must be eager, to be earnest and careful with all goodness and Excellence with praise upon our lips. To have knowledge with self-control enduring the gospel of Christ with love one to another as we are to love our heavenly Father with the same love which is charity, which suffers long.

Proverbs 3:11-13
My son, despise not the chastening of the Lord; neither be weary of his correction.
12th For whom the Lord loves he corrects, even as a father the son in whom he delights.
13th Happy is the man that finds **Wisdom**, and the man that gets understanding:

A father loves his child before the child is ever born, they make preparation, get the nursery painted and set up with all accessories, to await the promise of the baby's arrival. Then when the child is presented to the father, there is a bond of love that takes place immediately. There are no words to explain the love of a parent that starts the moment they find they are with child. When the child grows he gets corrected little bit here little bit there. They start out by saying no, then a tap on the hand. Then the child starts walking they get in things that can be harmful, the parent either removes them or the item out of the way of the child. Then as he grows the correction becomes harder for the lessons of life are harder. If we do not correct and teach the child he will not grow up into maturity he will have become fundamentally handicapped. The child will have become mentally handicapped if we do not work with the child. We must provide a place of safety as he learns or he/she will injure him/herself or possibly be killed. Through life's correction he matures into adulthood making his own way in life. Hopefully, we will be looking to the Lord for guidance. This is the way it is with our heavenly Father. Our heavenly Father corrects us, gives us **Wisdom**, to know we understand the correction of our Father. We are to look up to our Father, seek all what our Father has for us. We shall find the spirit of truth and it will lead us in all his truth. We want to grow up in the Lord as a mature Son. **Instruction** (Hebrew) correction, **Wisdom**, and teaching that imply correcting, and behavior, chastening, discipline, rebuke

Colossians 1:28-29
Whom we preach, warning every man, and teaching every man in all ***WISDOM;*** teaching and admonishing one another in psalms and hymns and spiritual songs, singing with Grace in your hearts to the Lord.

I Peter 4:17
For the time is come that MUST begin at the House of God: and if it first begin at us, what shall the end be of them that obey not the gospel of God.

Ephesians 3:10-11
To the intent that now unto the principalities and powers in heavenly places might be known by the church the MANIFOLD **WISDOM** OF GOD!
11th According to the eternal purposed in Christ Jesus our Lord.
Manifold (Greek) Various kinds, all kinds, many sided, diverse

Manifold **Wisdom** of God is many different ways that we can use **Wisdom**. There are various ways to walk in **Wisdom**. There are many sides to **Wisdom**, as there are many sides to a person, yet still only one person. Let's take a person in general. They are first a son or daughter. Then they are a husband or wife. They can become a parent, a teacher, a minister or a grandparent, etc. However, they are still the same person. They have a name. It takes a name to make any legal contract, to be legal and binding. This is what **Wisdom** is---many sides and many kinds; yet the same person, **Wisdom**. There is the **Wisdom** to raise a child, there is the **Wisdom** to run a church, there is the **Wisdom** to run a household, there is **Wisdom** on the job, there is the **Wisdom** to know when to speak and when to be quiet. We must have **Wisdom** to speak in the knowledge of God in any situation we encounter in our walk with the Lord.

St. John 16:13
Howbeit when the spirit of truth is come, he will guide you into all truth; for he shall not speak of himself, but whatsoever he shall hear, that she shall speak; and he will show you all things to come.

Proverbs 4:11-13
I have taught thee in the way of **Wisdom**; I have led thee in the right paths.

12th When thou goes, thy steps shall not be straightened; and when thou runs, thou shalt not stumble.
13th Take fast hold of instruction; let her not go; keep her; for she thy life.

Instruction (Hebrew) Correction, discipline, chastening, bond, **Wisdom** and teaching that imply correcting errant behavior, doctrine.

Take a hold of discipline, do not let go, instruction will teach you give life through correction. Your steps will strengthen and you will not stumble, for you have been taught **Wisdom**, for **Wisdom** will lead you in paths of righteousness. Discipline will cause you to mature, you will behave according to the Word of God. The spirit will lead you and to guide you, the spirit will cause you to grow and to be disciplined, your desires will change, your thoughts will change, as you mature in the Lord. But the Lord changes not.

I Kings 3:5
In Gibeon the Lord appeared to Solomon in a dream by night: and God said, ask what I shall give thee.

I Kings 3:9-10
Give therefore thy servant an understanding heart to judge thy people that I may discern between good and bad; for who is able to judge this thy so great a people.
10th And the speech pleased the Lord, that Solomon had asked this thing.
11th And God said unto him, because thou hast asked this thing, and hast not asked for thyself long life, neither asked for riches for thyself, nor asked the life of thine enemies; but hast asked for thyself understanding to discern .

Solomon was granted to ask God for anything he desired. Solomon did not ask for anything to please himself (**Flesh**). Solomon asked for something money could not and cannot buy, he asked for ***WISDOM! Knowledge With Understanding with discernment*** also to help his people. He had a love for his people and love for all mankind. There was a drawing of people to come even Kings came from everywhere, they came to hear of his great **Wisdom**. Solomon had the **Wisdom** to give a righteous judgment to his people. He knew how to discern the truth versus a lie and to know the good from the bad.

I Kings 3:23-28
Then said the king, The one said, This is my son that lives, and thy son is dead the dead: and the other said, nay; but thy son is dead, and my son is the living.
24th And the King said, bring me a sword, and they brought him a sword before the king.
25th And the King said, Divide the living child in two, and give half to the one, and half to the other.
26th Then spake the woman whose the living child was unto the king, for her bowels yearned upon her son, and she said, O my Lord, give her the living child, and in no wise slay it. But the other said, let it be neither mine nor thine, but divide it.
27th the king answered and said, give her the living child, and in no wise slay it; she is the mother thereof.
28th And all Israel heard of the which the king had judged; and they feared the king; for they saw that the **Wisdom** of God was in him to do.

This is true. This is true **Wisdom** straight from God above. This is where you see great **Wisdom** and discernment to understand to know the truth. He could have had the situation to go all wrong if he did not ask for such great **Wisdom** and discernment to help his people. An innocent child's life could have died.

I Kings 4:29-34
And God gave Solomon ***WISDOM*** and ***Understanding*** exceeding much, and largeness of heart, even as the sand that is on the sea shore.
34th And there came of all people to hear the ***WISDOM*** of Solomon from all kings of the earth, which heard of his **WISDOM**.

II Chronicles 9:22
And King Solomon passed all the kings of the earth in riches and ***WISDOM***.

Matthew 12:42; and Luke 11:31
The Queen of the South shall rise up in with this generation, and shall condemn it; for she came from the uttermost parts of the earth to hear the ***WISDOM;*** of Solomon and behold (**Look**) a ***GREATER THAN SOLOMON IS HERE!***
Queen (Hebrew) Wife of a king, with very high status, but not equal status, queen of heaven.

Isaiah 61:1-2
The spirit of the Lord is upon me; because the Lord hath anointed me to preach good tidings unto the meek; he hath sent me to bind up the broken hearted to proclaim liberty to the captives, and the opening of the prison to them that are bound.
2nd To proclaim the acceptable year of the Lord, and the day of vengeance of our God; to comfort to all that mourn.
Meek (Hebrew) humble, afflicted, poor, oppressed. Pleasure.
Comfort (Hebrew) repent, change one's mind, consoled.

The Lord Jesus came to give the good news; he came to save those who were lost. He came to the humble, the afflicted, to the poor to announce and appoint freedom to the ones that are held prisoners to the flesh. To set free the ones who are in bondage to religion of man. To announce the accepted time of the Lord. To the day of vengeance of our God to change one's mind to repent, to have a changed mind set; to be comforted when you are all alone, feel forsaken.

Isaiah 11: 1-2
And there shall come forth a ROD out of the STEM of Jesse, and A branch shall GROW out of his ROOTS.
2nd And the spirit shall rest upon him, the spirit of **Wisdom** and understanding, the spirit of counsel and might, the spirit of knowledge and of fear (reverence) of the Lord.
Stem (Hebrew) Root,
Rod (Hebrew) A shoot, twig,
Branch (Hebrew) A plant, shoot,
Counsel (Hebrew) Advise, purpose, plan.

There came forth a root out of a twig of Jesse, in other words, He came forth out of the loins of his Father Jesse, a plant or a shoot to grow out of his stem or roots, a seed. He came through the lineage of the tribe of Judah; which means praise. He came to earth with great ***Wisdom And Understanding,*** with a spirit of; advise, purpose, and a plan. We must see the need to have reverence of the Lord.

St. Luke 2:40.46-47, 52
And the child grew, and waxed strong in spirit, filled with ***WISDOM:*** and the ***GRACE of God*** was upon him.
46th And it came to pass, that after ***three days*** they found him in the temple, sitting in the midst of the doctor's, both hearing them, and asking them Questions.

47th And all that heard him were astonished at his understanding and answers.
52nd And Jesus increased in **Wisdom and Stature,** and in favor with God and man.

Jesus Christ as a young child of twelve (divine law and order) years old separated himself from his earthly parents to go do his Father's business. He was not worried about what his earthly parent would say or do. His mother asked him; why he was separated from them, for they looked for three days and could not find him. When his mother asked him why, he told her he must be about his Father's business. For **Jesus, being filled with Wisdom and Grace** was in the temple giving the word and ministering unto the elders. **Stature** (Greek) height or full grown.

Luke 4:18-21 (Jesus Speaking)
"The spirit of the Lord is upon me, because he hath anointed me to preach the gospel to the poor; he hath sent me to heal the broken hearted, to preach deliverance to the captives, and recovering of the sight to the blind, to set at liberty them that are bruised."
19th To preach the acceptable year of the Lord.
20th And he closed the book, and gave it to the minister, and set down. And the eyes of all them that were in the synagogue were fastened on him.
21st **And he began to say to them (Jesus Speaking), "_THIS DAY IS THIS SCRIPTURE FULFILLED IN YOUR EARS._"**

We see here that GREATER than Solomon is here! His name is Jesus Christ. He came to earth to redeem mankind back to God. He is the fulfillment of law; we are no longer under the law. We were condemned under the law. All the law did was condemn us and to bring death upon us. He went into the temple when he was twelve; he fulfilled the prophecy of Isaiah when he quoted Isaiah 61:1-2.

So we see here **Wisdom** builds her house, where creation is groaning and having an earnest desire to bring forth the Kingdom of his dear Son.

II Corinthians 5:1-2
For we know that if our earthly house of this tabernacle were dissolved, we have a building of God, an house not made with hands, eternal in the heavens.
2nd For in this we grown, earnestly desiring to be clothed upon with our house which is from heaven.

Revelation 3:18
I counsel thee to buy of me gold tried in the fire (Holy Ghost and with fire) that thou may be rich; and white raiment. That thou may clothed, and that the shame of thy nakedness do not appear; and thou may see.

We are to be no longer naked, we are to be clothed in his righteousness, we are the gold tried in the fires of cleansing, we are of Father God, rich in his love, and in his pure white robe of his great righteousness. When we are purged we take on the nature of the Father; we will no longer be of the old Adam nature we have taken on Jesus Christ and him crucified we will be the eternal tabernacle of God where he takes his abode.

Remember he was wounded in the house of his friends; We are just as guilty as the one who crucified him, for we were guilty, sin stained, and lost, we needed washed in the precious Lamb of God's blood, for life is in the blood.

St. John 1:29
The next day John sees Jesus coming to him, and said; BEHOLD (LOOK) THE LAMB OF GOD, which taketh away the sins of the world.

John was prophesied in the Old Testament he was coming in the spirit of Elijah the prophet to be the fore-runner of Jesus Christ, no greater man than John the Baptist for he Introduced Jesus to the World.

Then shortly after, John was beheaded. For John was the end of the law and Jesus is Grace; and law and Grace cannot walk hand in hand. John represented the Law and Jesus came to give GRACE! The law was not done away with; but Jesus fulfilled the law.

Notes

Questions and Answers

1. Who is **Wisdom**?

2. How do you gain **Wisdom**?

3. What is a balance?

4. We are to get **Wisdom**, _____, and Understanding.

5. What is a fool, scoffer and a sluggard?

6. How many stories high was the Ark?

7. What was Moses laid in and placed in the water?

8. How long did his mother hide him?

9. Into what tribe was Moses born in?

10. Who did Ruth marry?

11. Esther was whose adopted daughter.

12. Who was King David's father?

13. Why did Samuel go to the house of Jesse?

14. King David had how many brothers?

15. How many days was Jonah in Hell?

16. Who was the fore-runner of Jesus Christ?

17. What does the word, Behold mean?

18. Who was wounded in the house of their friends?

19. Why was John beheaded

20. What did Jesus come to fulfill?

21. What did **Wisdom** build?

22. Who is **Wisdom**?

23. What does three mean?

24. What does Seven mean?

25. Who was Boaz in the Book of Ruth?

Notes

For Seminars or Revivals please Contact The Prophet Sandra Crum at Sandra.crum1956@yahoo.com

Printed in the United States
By Bookmasters